Let Our Children Soar!

The Complexity and Possibilities of Educating the English Language Student

Bolgen Vargas, Ed.D.

First published 2023

by John Catt Educational Ltd
15 Riduna Park, Station Road,
Melton, Woodbridge, IP12 1QT, UK
Tel: +44 (0) 1394 389850

4500 140th Ave North,
Suite 101, Clearwater,
FL 33762-3848, US
Tel: +1 561 448 1987

Email: enquiries@johncatt.com
Website: www.johncatt.com

ISBN: 978 1 398388 67 3

Set and designed by John Catt Educational Limited

"By telling his own personal story, as an immigrant and English language learner, Bolgen Vargas vividly illustrates how teachers and school environments can tap into a young person's motivations and help them "soar," as he says, to their full potential. In addition to his inspiring story, Bolgen encourages us to examine the limitations in our school systems and think about how we, as educators, can influence meaningful change that supports both students and teachers. This book is a must read for all teachers and school administrators."

Dr. Adam Urbanski, President of the Rochester Teachers Association and Vice President of the American Federation of Teachers

"Let Our Children Soar! is powerful. For students, this book is a memoir filled with hope and inspiration. Imagine the classroom discussions that would occur as students wrestle with immigration, language, perseverance and opportunity! For teachers and administrators, it is a case study to open opportunities for reflection, discourse and application. This book will leave a lasting impact on all who read it."

Ellen Tuohey, Elementary Teacher

"I wish every teacher, every school administrator who is working with k-12 immigrants and their families would read this book. It is touching, invigorating and an excellent resource for deeper discussions and reflection on the power of educators and the potential for each student to soar."

Dr. Vicma Ramos, Superintendent of Wayne-Finger Lakes Boces, former ELL teacher

"Bolgen Vargas' journey from his youth in a rural Caribbean community with little or no access to formal education to becoming a progressive educational leader in the United States is fascinating, compelling, and inspirational. He writes with the voice of one who understands the struggles so many of our English language learning students undergo. While too often educational philosophies that focus on assimilation and filling in perceived deficits drive "education reform," Bolgen demands that we approach our teaching with a lens of asset-based pedagogy. Though this book is more a personal narrative than a how-to manual, it offers priceless advice on working with English language learners and the importance of relationship building between teachers and counselors and our students."

Dr. Ellen Bernstein, President, Albuquerque Teachers Federation

"The Bolgen Vargas I've known as his former high school English teacher has not really changed much over the years. He has always grabbed chances despite the odds against his succeeding. Imagine: staying in a class way too advanced for his circumstance, going to an out of town college where he earned bachelor and masters degrees, becoming superintenent of schools in two different states, getting a doctorate in education from a prestigious university, writing this book, and most of all maintaining my daughter's and my friendship for over 45 years. As a retired teacher I look forward to seeing Bolgen's book in print. It will open educators' eyes to a whole new amazing world. Finally, this book is a tribute to all the educators and students who have struggled with a new language, a new country and new customs."

Judith Goldberg, Retired English Teacher, Seward Park High School

You probably have heard the saying, "Each of us has one book within us." For many years I heard from friends and colleagues that I should write a book about my immigrant experience. They seemed to believe, well before I did, that I had something unique to share, and I was given enough encouragement that I thought seriously about what I would say. As I often am inclined to do, I talk about an idea and share my thinking with others, in this case mostly my wife, Jill. So after more than 10 years of pondering the possibility, and as we were facing the beginnings of the Covid pandemic, Jill finally confronted me with, "It's not a book unless its written!" This book, therefore, sprang from the support and encouragement (the kick in the pants) that Jill gave me. Indeed, she became my first editor.

I dedicate the book to Jill, to my mother and father, and to my brother Arsenio and his wife Ydalia for the sacrifices they made to bring me to America to pursue the American dream, and to all my siblings. Also, I dedicate this to all the teachers and professors who never gave up on me even when I was ready to do so myself. Finally, there are simply too many people to mention who supported me along the way and, indeed, put the wind beneath my wings so that I might soar.

Bolgen Vargas' life began in a small rural hamlet in the Dominican Republic where he walked barefoot to school or, on a lucky day, rode on the back of a donkey. As a teenager without any knowledge of the English language he transitioned to the bewildering environment of New York City to join his mother. He beat the odds that his beginnings would have predicted by graduating from high school. A graduate of SUNY Brockport and from the University of Pennsylvania, GSE, he spent his entire career educating children from all walks of life. He served as Superintendent of the Rochester, NY School District and the Manchester, NH School District.

Acknowledgements

I am hugely indebted to Jud Mead for helping to make this book possible, for sharing his special editorial talent and using his wonderful curiosity to pose questions that pushed me to tell my story deeper. Our many conversations, over the phone, by email and during many lunches, not only enhanced the stories but was akin to personal therapy. For his time spent with me, I also thank Jud's wife, Debbie, for her patience and support. I am grateful for Jud's tireless editing and his belief in the project from the first draft to the last. Finally, I am ultimately grateful that this project brought to me this kind and wonderful person who has become a valued friend for life.

Special thanks go to Ellen Tuohey for reading each one of the many drafts of this book. As an elementary school teacher, she provided valuable insight about the work of teachers each and every day.

To Carlos Garcia, for reading the manuscript, offering insight, and writing the foreword to this book. Carlos was one of the first people to encourage me to become an administrator.

And to Gary Craig, for sharing his experience and expertise on drafting a book proposal.

I owe much gratitude to the following people who read an early or final draft of the manuscript: Judy Goldberg, Eve Donahue, Rosemary Callard-Szulgit, Donna White, Laura Shackelford, Adam Urbanski, Delio Collado, Vicki Ramos, Karina Vargas, Larry and Robin Frye, Luis Perez, Pamela Perez, Cathy Reef, Leslie Goldberg, Ann Mitchell, Ellen Bernstein, Walter Cooper. They gave generously of their time and provided important feedback that helped to shape this book.

I also want to acknowledge the people that I have had the good fortune to work with over the years and who helped to shape my experience:

- First, my teachers, counselors and administrators who received me at Seward Park High School, the first institution and set of teachers in America who added meaning to my life.

- My colleagues and staff at Puerto Rican Youth Development (PRYD), particularly Roberto Burgos and Margaret Sanchez who also brought me to the Rochester Educational Opportunity Center to work with adult students and mentored me early in my career.

- To all my colleagues at Greece Arcadia High School, particularly the counseling team of Sandy Tidings, Rick Worner, Danielle Fico, Sheila Evans, Ron Zimarino; Mary Champagne-Meyers and the rest of the foreign language teachers who always fed me lunch; the English department, particularly Patty Goodwin who became a life-long friend; Sam Fico from the business department; and the secretaries who gave me so much support including Sharon Rich, Sue Hulbert, Kathy Antosh, and Sandy Bubel.

- Special thanks to all my students at Greece Arcadia who helped me grow as a person and an educator.

- To SUNY Brockport faculty, staff and peers, for opening the opportunity to experience a whole new world. Special thanks to the Educational Opportunity Program (EOP) faculty and staff and to Marsha Gottovi, director of admissions, who admitted me based on "my potential" and hired me for my first work study job.

- The faculty of the graduate program in Counselor Education, particularly Dr. Jeremiah Donigian who was my advisor and challenged me to the bone. For that I thank him!

- The faculty of the University of Pennsylvania Graduate School of Education Mid-Career Doctoral Program in Educational Leadership, particularly my dissertation committee: Michael Nakkula, Sharon Ravitch and fellow student and colleague Jana Carlisle; Michael Johanek, Senior Fellow, Graduate School of Education, Director Mid-Career Doctoral Program in Educational Leadership and my peers in the program who offered their encouragement and support.

- Special thanks to Arthur Beaudry and Leslie Want, as well as others in the Manchester School District and community for welcoming this unlikely outsider to serve as Superintendent.
- Thanks, too, to the Rochester School District staff and community for adopting me as one of their own.
- I want to thank a number of people I met when I was fresh out of college, who saw in me leadership potential and pushed me to serve as a leader in the Latino community and later to run for elective office: Sue Costa, Nancy Padilla, Juan Padilla, Luz Padilla, Belen Colon, Father Tracy, Pedro Maneiro, Relton Roland, Pete Otero, Judy Kerr, Jim Rice, Jack Queen, David Gant, Manny Rivera, Julio Vasquez, John Rodriguez, Nydia Padilla Rodriguez, Lynn Barber, Eugenio Marlin and so many others too long to list.

To Jaci Ayorinde, for her feedback and artist eye.

Special thanks to Mark Combes, Director of North America for John Catt Educational, for guiding me from the beginning to the end of this book, his general editing, and support without which this book would not have been possible.

To Dr. Walter Cooper, scientist, Civil Rights leader, NYS Regent Emeritus, and my long-time friend and mentor, whose insights and experiences have helped me develop as an educational leader.

I want to end where I started: to acknowledge my wife and our beloved dogs, Tesoro and Lindo, for their unconditional love and support.

Contents

Foreword: By Carlos A Garcia 13

Chapter 1: This little boy might come to your school 15

Chapter 2: You know where you were born 29

Chapter 3: America came to us before we came to America 41

Chapter 4: Waiting, hoping, and radio school 55

Chapter 5: From the hamlet to Seward Park High School 67

Chapter 6: How did that happen? 83

Chapter 7: Hope and possibility 101

Chapter 8: The place of common sense in education reform 121

FOREWORD
By Carlos A Garcia

Imagine one of your former English Language Leaner students taking you on his journey. You learn where he came from, how he came to your school, where he went after he graduated. How much would you benefit from the opportunity to see his multiple worlds from his eyes?

Bolgen Vargas takes us on such a journey. He tells the story of how his life began in a small rural *pueblecito* (hamlet) in the Dominican Republic. When he immigrates to New York City, he finds himself navigating the challenges of a new world. Bolgen shares this wonderful account of his own life experiences as a catalyst for motivating teachers, administrators and educational institutions to better understand the immigrant experience. And he uses his story to illustrate common sense approaches to education that might better serve students' needs.

His story emphasizes the fundamental importance of understanding our children's backgrounds if we are going to be successful in educating them. He describes how easily the immigrant population experience is either ignored or only dealt with through a deficit model, arguing that language and zip code should not be the primary determining factor in student outcomes. The immigrant experience is a rich and wonderful asset that, if understood, can be incorporated into instruction to help maximize student success. His own experience of language challenges as an immigrant clearly demonstrates that we as educators should never misinterpret not knowing English as a criterion in determining a student's intellect.

Bolgen's journey of transformation from dirt-floor poverty in the Dominican Republic to becoming an urban school superintendent in the U.S. exemplifies what the American dream is all about. The strength and will that this immigrant brought with him, should serve as a reminder to all of us that our support and understanding in our classrooms can truly open the future for immigrants.

Bolgen is an innovator in education. He has taken all his life challenges and incorporated them into action plans to address not only migrant education, but all education and community-based issues. He understands the complexity of issues in education today and remains intent and focused on bringing about effective change. He is a leader in community-based solutions and knows that change needs to come from within, with the direct involvement of all the stakeholders. His work should reinforce the attitude that educators need to be better listeners and need to "walk the talk." Education is what we work to make it and it can only be improved by us, The Educators.

As its title suggests, this book tells a story that provides hope and possibility. It will inspire you in your commitment to support all students to reach their full potential, and give you insights and ideas to put into practice as a school teacher, administrator and K-12 educator.

Carlos A Garcia, Superintendent (retired), San Francisco, CA, Unified School District.

Chapter 1

This little boy might come to your school

"I am what time, circumstance, history, have made of me, certainly, but I am, also, much more than that. So are we all."

James Baldwin

It was a late spring afternoon in 2010, and I was in my first week as interim superintendent of the Rochester City School District. The district was in crisis, which included the layoff of more than 600 teachers, and I was holding a series of meetings with school administrators and teachers to share with them and engage them in how we would be addressing the challenges. I was speaking with district assistant principals in a large conference room in one of the schools. When I ended my presentation, a petite Latina woman who looked vaguely familiar came up to me, clearly shaken and with tears in her eyes. "Do you remember me? I'm here because of you."

I did remember. She'd been one of my students in an Educational Opportunity Center pilot program to help bilingual single mothers move from welfare to work where I'd worked as a young college graduate. She told me that whenever she'd been discouraged, I'd always encouraged her. Now she was a vice principal in a district school. She gave me a big hug.

She had come far. As it happens, so had I.

15

When I was six, I had not yet held a pencil, but I was agile and strong enough to climb the mango, avocado, and tamarind trees on our farm. I could spot the ripest and sweetest mango, climb to it, hold onto a branch with one hand, and pick the fruit with the other. My greatest joy was to get the sweetest mangos for my mother and grandmother, who lived with us. They would say, "*Gracias, este es el mango mas dulce* (Thank you, this is the sweetest mango)."

My father, in his grumpy way, could care less about mangos, but he cared very much about avocados—especially a big, ripe, creamy one. He'd never say "Gracias" when I brought him one. But I knew he was pleased.

Jesús María Vargas Cruz, my father, was known to everyone as María. According to family lore, my grandmother, who we called Mama, had added the female name because she'd wanted a daughter.

Although María was very strong, I knew by his bald head and missing teeth that he was old. He didn't find humor in life, and his temperament, at least in my child's world, made him someone to fear. He knew only farming and how to make his *café*. He drank coffee all day from sunrise to sunset.

The one crop my father never sold was his coffee beans. The plot where he grew coffee was too small. If you came by our *bohio* (a small, thatched-roof dwelling) at exactly noon, my father would be making coffee, and at 4 p.m. he would make his last pot of the day. He roasted his beans with sugar in a special iron pot that had been passed on to him by my grandfather. But he believed that the most important factor for making good coffee was a coffee strainer made of cotton cloth. This was the old way of making coffee, and for my father it was the only way.

To me, everything seemed like the only way. For generations, my family had been born in the backcountry hamlet of Boca de Cabía in the region of Puerto Plata in the Dominican Republic about 140 miles northwest of the capital, Santo Domingo.

Boca de Cabía sits on fertile land blessed by tropical rains sufficient for subsistence farming and to fill the Bajabonico and the Caonao rivers that gave us our fresh water. It seemed like we had sunshine 365 days a year and enough flowers year-round to please the heart and feed the bees that made the sweetest honey. And although it was poor, our hamlet, with its population of fewer than 100 people, provided most of our basic needs and everything I wanted. This was my world, beautiful and complete, between its two rivers.

The hamlet was a scattering of farms along a dirt road connecting it to three nearby towns. From this road you see lush rolling hills with palms, mangos, avocados, lemons, and oranges among the woods and fields.

People in the village lived, for the most part, in small huts along the road, set back on little plots of farmland—this is how my family lived. A few houses in the hamlet were more substantial, built of palm board, colorfully painted, with metal roofs and concrete floors. These houses had more land, and cows and cattle in the fields, which were signs of greater wealth. Having cows ensures milk to sell and from that at least some predictable income for the family.

In the hamlet, for most of the families, including mine, the day is taken up with working on the farm and tending to day-to-day tasks such as getting water, taking care of the animals, finding food, fishing in the rivers, and sometimes traveling by horse to the ocean about 20 miles away to fish.

We didn't have much in terms of what one would consider material goods or modern things, such as electricity, but we had enough energy supplied for free by the sun and the moon. On a dark night I always felt the energy of the stars as they blanketed the sky. Nature found its way to warm the heart, humble us, and make us appreciate what very little we did have. And even though our table wasn't large enough for the family to sit with friends and talk about our joys and sorrows, we had a large mango tree where we could sit and carry on those conversations in its cool shade.

We may not have had much, but I had a horse. He was born when I was eight, and I called him Rainbow. We knew each other like soul mates. He was Rainbow only to me. We didn't recognize our animals with names but referred to them by description—white horse, black horse.

We ate our meals and gathered for conversation on a dirt patio next to the open-air kitchen shaded by the tall mango tree with lush green leaves that had been there forever. Everyone in the family, even my grandmother, remembered her when they were growing up just as she was now. She had

17

magically survived all the violent winds that blew through her. She was good to me when I was hungry, dropping ripe kidney-shaped mangos ready to eat. I would peel the overripe fruit and then bite in and slurp the sweet pulp, the juice running down my chin.

Our small *bohio* was made of royal palm boards with a thatch roof of royal palm leaves and sticks on beams. It had two rooms: a small living room with a table in the center where we did our schoolwork, and a large bedroom with three beds where we all slept. My mother and father shared their bed with me. I never thought that was unusual. It was all I'd ever known.

My mother and father

We were always in bed when darkness settled on the hamlet. Whereas the days were filled with activity and the blended sounds of the animals neighing, lowing, cackling, bleating and wheezing, the nights slowly quieted down to a hush. Even the birds settled after dark. You might hear frogs and the sounds of an owl, but you did not hear voices as the hamlet slept. Most nights, the air was soft with fresh fragrance from the mangos, guavas, and the ever-present wildflowers.

On moonless nights in the winter months, when night fell at 6 p.m., the stars were almost the only lights in the hamlet, a perfect blanket across the sky. The meager light from our one kerosene lamp did not compete with the vast night sky of stars. Occasionally, a kerosene lamp glowed faintly from the doorway of the one other *bohio* we could see, high above us on a hillside. Otherwise, we saw no light except what came from the night sky.

I was the youngest of eight children spanning 20 years. When my earliest memories begin, some of my brothers and sisters had already left home. The oldest, my sister Luz, was living in the capital, already married, when I was born. Arsenio, my second oldest brother, had left the hamlet to work in the capital when I was too young to remember. He had begun to help support the rest of our family by the time he was 12 years old. Elpidio had joined the Dominican navy. So I was growing up with my sisters Holanda and Pujinga and my brothers Digno and Papalo.

In the mornings we scrambled in different directions. Holanda was off to the one-room school for two hours of instruction. My brothers might be on their way to the fields or to the market in Imbert or Luperón or the city of Puerto Plata to sell our plantains, bananas, cassavas, avocados, oranges, mangos, chickens, pigs, and goats. The rest of us would take care of the animals, carry water from the river, and work the crops.

I couldn't wait to turn seven so I could go to school. Holanda liked learning—she would be the first in our family to graduate from high school after she moved to the capital. Before I was old enough to go to school, I watched her trying to teach my father and mother how to read. She made some progress with my father: she taught him to sign his name and to read basic sentences. Unfortunately, she didn't succeed with my mother. At the end of her long life, my mother died without understanding the written word at all. She was strong and brilliant in her environment, but she couldn't sign her name. I am still haunted by that.

Noon meant two things in our household: my father making his coffee and my father arguing with my mother.

As soon as he had poured his coffee, my father and my mother and anyone else who was there would sit under the mango tree next to the kitchen. I recall arguments about various matters, but none was as regular or more heated than about my mother's determination that her sons and daughters should move from the *campos* (fields) to the capital as soon as they could.

"You were born poor here in the *campos* but you don't have to die here," my mother would say. "There is a better life to be had than the hard life on the *conucos* (plot of farmland)."

"Stop poisoning our children with your stupid idea that they will be better off by moving to the capital than staying here helping us work the farm," my father would yell.

I was seven or eight. I had heard this exchange over and over again.

"Look at Luz," my mother would say. "Because I helped her move to the capital, she's now married to a good man and they have two beautiful children and they do well. If she hadn't gone, God knows where she would be."

My mother would talk of my brothers who'd left the farm. Elpidio had joined the Dominican navy with the help of Luz's husband. Arsenio had left to work with his uncle Edilio at his bar. Then he went to work for "the Chinese" and they were good to him because he was a hard worker. He was saving money and helping us.

"Every month Arsenio sends us a box full of food and a few pesos. He would not be better off working here on the farm. He wouldn't have a penny in his pocket working here with you. We can't save a penny ourselves. There isn't time for our children to go to school because they are always working. We have very little here."

"*Little!*" My father bellows the word. "Look at Luperón and Imbert! *They* have little! So they have electricity and they have a paved road, but they don't have much else. If it weren't for us working on the farms, they wouldn't have anything to eat! And the capital? They don't even have enough water there. So what good is it to have the things you say but they don't have water?"

"Look at me," my mother says. "I work like crazy. My father and my grandparents worked like crazy, with nothing to show for it but the small amount of land we have. I wanted to go to school and learn lots of things, like reading, but I couldn't because I had to work at home. I want more for my children. So stop trying to stop me, because no one can stop me. Only God can stop me."

20

We all worked hard. Like most villages in the countryside, then and now, we did not have running water or wells. My sisters and my mother were responsible for carrying all the water we used from the river. My brothers and I brought the large animals to the river to drink. But my sisters and my mother carried water in large buckets on their heads for the pigs, chickens, ducks, and turkeys and of course water for cooking, drinking, and other needs. They washed our clothes at the rivers.

I asked my mother, "How are you able to carry so much water and smoke a cigar at the same time?"

"Very simple," she said. "Women are made much stronger than men from head to toe."

The boys swam naked in the river to bathe and dried naked under the radiant Caribbean sun, cooled by the gentle river breeze. The girls did the same in their own bend of the river. We didn't have electricity or running water, but we had the rivers and the sun.

Octavia, my mother, was a small woman with long salt-and-pepper hair, a big smile, and an even bigger heart who always spoke her mind. She'd known nothing but poverty and she was determined that her children would do better. The only way she could see this happening was through education, which would require us to leave our hamlet.

One sunny, hot afternoon, after arguing with my father, my mother walked rapidly to where I was watching my brother Papalo plow land with oxen to sow cassavas in our small *cunuco*.

My mother began whispering to him. I desperately wanted to hear what she was saying, but I didn't dare approach them. She spoke for about five minutes and my brother spoke just a few words, nodding his head. I was sure he responded with the same word: *sí, sí, sí, sí*, and *sí*.

"I need to speak with you secretly about something very serious and very important."

I was certain that was how she'd started the conversation because my brother appeared nervous, and after the conversation ended he could not keep the bulls plowing straight.

21

My guess was confirmed when we went to bed at our customary time of 8 p.m., just after sunset. I was nestled between my parents at night. I heard my mother speaking very quietly to my father.

"Not even the dictator Trujillo could stop me from getting my children to a better place," she said. "Trujillo tried to keep all of us in the countryside with his laws. He is dead. But even if he were resurrected, he could not stop me."

My father replied with the softest and most gentle voice I ever heard him use.

"If Trujillo were alive, you could never say that," he said. "You and the whole family would be killed by the regime. He was a bad man, but he did establish good law and order so that the *campesinos* (farmers) could not all move from the countryside to cities without the permission of the government."

It was very hot again the next afternoon. Papalo and Digno had returned from Imbert, where they had gone to sell 10 quintals of yuccas. I was with my father at the pig corral giving them water because they were suffering from the heat. I couldn't wait to see whether Papalo and Digno had brought the sweet bread they bought when they had a good day at the market.

It had been a good day. They'd brought home the bread I craved, three pounds of rice, and a bottle of the lard that we used for all cooking. We hardly ever cooked with oil because we didn't produce it in our hamlet and it was too expensive for us. I always felt privileged when we were able to afford the sweet bread made outside the hamlet rather than cassava bread, which was what we ate every day.

It stopped being a good day for me at four in the afternoon when Papalo didn't show up at the baseball field. We were now short a player who might make the difference between winning and losing the game—a game we'd bet 15 cents on and, more important, our pride, which is always tied to every baseball game.

"Where's Papalo?"

Digno's lips were tight. "I am going to catch. Just throw strikes, and try not to let your hand shake so much."

Since early childhood I'd had a tremor that made people think I was nervous and that I couldn't pitch. I could hear the taunts from the other team, "He's shaking like an old man!" but I knew that I could put the ball where I wanted.

We played without Papalo. Everyone was surprised that he was missing—except Digno.

"Where were you?" I asked Papalo when I found him at home.

"I went to the river to fish and caught five tilapias." Indeed, he had.

My mother cooked a dinner of tilapia, *guisada* (a type of stew), and *platanos* (plantains).

During dinner, Papalo was quieter than usual. I knew something was going on that he didn't want to reveal to me. I knew he would run away to the capital with my mother's support. It was just a matter of time. And that was likely very soon. There has to be a better reason than fishing for a Dominican to miss a baseball game. I was not such a child as to believe that he would skip playing baseball to go fishing all by himself.

When we die, if we were to see two trails, one leading to heaven and the other to a baseball game, most Dominicans would follow the trail to the baseball game. I knew that Papalo, Digno, and all the boys I grew up with hoped baseball could be our bridge to America and our way out of poverty.

My mother disagreed. The way to prosperity was education and hard work—and to move from the countryside to the capital.

My mother was not about to accept a fate driven by circumstance. She wanted us to be much more than that which our history and circumstances would dictate.

Why tell this story?

I have described some of my early childhood experience because I want you to know where I came from as a student—as the kind of student you may meet one day or likely already know. I don't intend to suggest that my experience and my family circumstances are representative of all English language learner (ELL) students—just this one.

However, there are several things in my young experience I do share with many other ELLs: poverty, eagerness to learn, lack of books at home, the inability of parents to help me with schoolwork and language, among others. In the next few chapters, I will tell you more about my family and my adolescent years and my evolution as a student, starting in my hamlet and eventually enrolling in a large New York City high school.

I know well that getting to know your students is not as easy as it sounds. I hope I can give you—teachers and administrators—useful insights into the complexity of getting to know ELLs coming, as they do, from different cultures, social classes, family circumstances, and immigrant experiences. I will cover much more in this book than the complexity of getting to know students and their families, but I will say here at the start that if we are serious as educators—and as an education system—about really knowing our students and their families, we need to look at the caseload and workload of teachers. Knowing our ELL students takes time, and teachers can't invent more time for themselves. The time they need must be made available.

In my capacity as a superintendent in urban school districts, I met well-meaning and genuinely concerned business leaders who wondered why educators are so challenged in helping their students succeed. Many assumed that getting to know our students is as easy as getting to know their customers. When I shared my story, many of these leaders experienced an *Aha* moment. There is a lot to know about a life! In the following chapters I will draw from research, ideas from experts in the field; my own expertise in public education; and my personal experience as an immigrant, student, educator, and community leader to provide you with thoughts about education that go beyond my own life and professional experience. It is my hope that you will also have some *Aha* moments along the way.

Reflect and Imagine Activity

Imagine that seven-year-old Bolgen showed up at your school. This seven-year-old Bolgen did not—that was not yet my fate—but thousands of children arrive in our schools every year just as innocent of any other way of life than the one they've known on their farms, or in refugee camps, or whatever utterly foreign existence that has been their only world until almost the minute you meet them.

Here are two likely scenarios.

As a teacher, you are fortunate that your school has a strong capacity to serve students like him. You take the first step that is required by federal law: school districts and charter schools must have a process to determine the language(s) spoken in each student's home and to objectively identify students who need language support services due to their limited proficiency in speaking, reading, writing, or understanding English.

You gave Bolgen the district English language assessment, and the result confirms that he doesn't know the alphabet in English or even in Spanish, his native language. It is clear that his home language is Spanish, and you are able to confirm that the first English language exposure this student had ever had was upon arrival at John F. Kennedy International Airport.

Your school offers three programs for you to consider to support young Bolgen.

English as a Second Language

English as a second language (ESL), beginners-level English, was developed as an alternative to the "sink-or-swim" approach. ESL stresses simplified speech and uses visual or physical cues, memorization, and drills. ESL can include several language groups in the same classroom. The goal is all about getting kids to function in English as quickly as possible and spend a minimal amount of time in a child's native language.

Transitional Bilingual

Bilingual has two goals: help the students to achieve English proficiency and continue instruction in their native language. Bilingual programs generally focus on Spanish speakers because they are the largest non–English-speaking group in public schools currently (approximately 70 percent of the ELL student population are Spanish speakers). In a bilingual classroom, the teacher must be bilingual, and all subjects, including math, science, and social studies, are taught in Spanish, but the focus is on English proficiency in writing and reading. The goal is to help students become fluent in two languages.

Dual Language

In this model, instruction should be split into two sections, with one part of the school day in English and the other in a different language. For this to work properly, the teacher(s) must be fluent in both languages. In a version of this model, often called dual immersion, ideally half of the class consists of non-native English speakers and half of native English speakers.

In which program would you place Bolgen?

In what grade level would you place him?

What are the strengths and challenges that Bolgen brings to school?

What school barriers do you think can get in the way of Bolgen's success?

As you reflect, what curricular, instructional, and assessment issues come to your mind?

Now consider that you and young Bolgen are not as lucky. You are in a school that does not have great resources for ELL students. Your school only offers one program, which is ESL. Also, you are in a community where many residents don't support the settlement of immigrants, a vocal minority of the school board believes that ELL students are too expensive to educate, and even some general education teachers seem reluctant to work with students learning ESL.

You have a district policy that states you must place according to the grade skills not by age, where social promotion is not allowed. There are only two teachers of ESL at your school. You speak very little Spanish and your other teachers of ESL only speak English.

What are the strengths and challenges that Bolgen brings to your school?

As you reflect, what curricular, instructional, and assessment issues come to your mind?

What school barriers do you think can get in the way of Bolgen's success?

The story of seven-year-old Bolgen, who has never held a pencil, may sound like that of some of the immigrant children you've seen in your classroom. The constructs of a school building, with its structures and expectations, may be unknown to this child and his family. Yet, a little knowledge about the environment they've come from helps you meet them where they are and this can open up a world of opportunity as you learn to unfold the hidden, unique skills and experiences these newcomers bring to their transition into a traditional classroom. Teachers and administrators can be most helpful when they come to understand the assets and potential the immigrant child brings rather than focusing on the deficits they face in the basic fundamentals, which are more evident.

In 2019 there were more than five million ELL students in the United States, which represents 10.4 percent of the K–12 student population (National Center for Education Statistics [NCES], 2022). Approximately 77 percent of ELL students are Hispanic. The top 10 most commonly reported home languages are as follows: Spanish, Arabic, English, Chinese, Vietnamese, Portuguese, Russian, Haitian Creole, Hmong, and Korean (NCES, 2022). Although these are the most commonly reported languages, the ELL student population is as diverse as the world, and meeting each and every one of them where they are is a teacher's greatest challenge.

Current federal, state, and local policies and practices, such as high-stakes testing, linking high-stakes testing to teacher evaluations, and rigid pacing guides, make this imperative doubly challenging. When devoted teachers and administrators are burdened by ill-conceived policies and practices such as these, the needs of the most vulnerable children get lost.

Reference

National Center for Education Statistics. (2022). *English learners in public schools.* US Department of Education, Institute of Education Sciences. https://nces.ed.gov/programs/coe/indicator/cgf

Chapter 2

You know where you were born

"When we are not able to change a situation, we are challenged to change ourselves."

Viktor E. Frankl

Right after dusk it began to pour, accompanied by lightning and thunder. It rained all night and the rivers would be rising, impossible to cross on foot. But that didn't stop my brother Papalo from running away to the capital as he and my mother planned.

I'd heard him go long before dawn, and this wasn't a market day. I was surprised he'd try to cross the river after such a rain, when it would be rising fast and flowing powerfully enough to sweep away the strongest mule. But I never thought Papalo wouldn't make it. Swimming across a swollen river was almost a necessary skill in our hamlet.

My father hadn't noticed Papalo leave. We got up at 5 a.m. as usual and I was full of dread for the fight between my mother and father certain to come, knowing that my brother and sisters and I would be in the middle.

"Where is Papalo?" María was sipping his morning coffee.

Everyone was silent. Not even my mother was brave enough to be the bearer of news that would infuriate María.

29

"Where is Papalo?" he asked again louder.

As if we were a choir, we answered precisely at the same instant with two words, "*No se*"—"Don't know."

My mother, on the other hand, didn't answer, not even with a nod of the head. She was as silent as my dry tears, except that her silence could not be hidden. It didn't take much time for María, who couldn't handle silence, to ask Octavia directly with his angriest and most forceful voice, "*¿Dónde está Papalo, el vagabundo?*"

Octavia responded, "*Gracias a Dios y la Virgin de la Altagracia*, he ran to the capital as he should to search for a better life."

María stood up in a rage and began berating my mother, even calling her "*una madre malisima*" (a dreadful mother). She didn't respond. No tears, no trembling, just silent bravery. My heart was bruised. In a strange way, I wished that my father could have gotten his way to keep Papalo and the rest of us in *el campo*. I kept my eyes dry and my tears secret.

My brother Digno and my sisters Patricia and Holanda were well versed in the struggle over a sibling's exodus. They didn't appear scared or saddened. They were actually full of joy inside and were repressing their feelings for the sake of appearing dutiful, as I was repressing my tears.

We were behaving exactly the way our father and mother expected; we were taught to be obedient above all. Respect your parents, elders, and teachers and don't contradict them by asking questions.

María ordered Digno to get a horse ready to go searching for Papalo. They rode away. However, the effort was in vain. The river was by now too high and the current too strong even for a very angry man to dare cross. He came back ranting. I wished he would stop, but the ranting continued for days.

My mother's silence, by contrast, gave me confidence that her plan for Papalo had succeeded. I knew that if anything had gone wrong, she would have received word from the driver she'd arranged to pick up Papalo at El Estrecho, the town on the paved road from the country to the capital. The driver, who had the only car for hire in our area, left for the capital every morning around 5:30. If Papalo hadn't made it to El Estrecho, we'd know.

So, I followed my mother's example and didn't worry that Papalo might not be safe.

Messages came to us in a variety of ways. We didn't have a telephone, of course, and our only electricity was the battery in the radio. Sometimes, if she had important information for us, my sister Luz would pay for a radio announcement: "*This message is for my mother, Octavia Vargas, from her daughter Luz in the capital. She has sent a letter and you can pick it up in Imbert.*" Imbert was about 12 miles from Boca de Cabía. For an urgent message, she could send a telegram to Imbert and send the message by radio for the family to pick it up *inmediatamente*.

There was no postal service to our hamlet. We usually relied on Don Buenita Cruz, the mayor of Boca de Cabía, to pick up the rare letter from the post office in Imbert and deliver it to us when he found time to visit, or to send word for us to retrieve it from him.

He brought a letter from Papalo about 10 days later.

My father had great respect for Don Buenita. When he arrived with the letter, María offered him coffee and they sat down to talk.

"You know, I wish that boy didn't run away to the capital where there is so much trouble. Life in the capital is not easy," my father said. "But most important I need him here to help maintain the family."

"*Don María,*" Don Buenita said, "*con el respeto debido usted esta equivocado.*"—With due respect, you are wrong.

"*¿Por que?*" María asked.

"You are wrong because if you and I were as young as your sons and daughters, we too would be looking to move from the campo to the capital or to another city."

Don Buenita said that every young person and now even old folks were leaving the campo to go to the capital to enjoy the benefits of progress they didn't have here.

"Ask yourself this, Don María: Why did all your family except for you and Panchin move to the capital? And aren't they all doing well?"

"Why are people from all over the country flooding from the countryside to the capital, to Santiago and other cities?" he asked. "Why do you think that all these people who went to the capital are not coming back?"

"Finally, Don María, *con respeto,* let me tell you that the only reason that you and Panchin are surviving in the campo with your family is because of your mother's inheritance of land," Don Buenita said. "The day she passes away, your brothers and sisters will come to sell their part of the inheritance and then you will be left without enough land to support your family."

My father looked straight into his eyes and, after a long silence, which is more characteristic of my mother, nodded his head slightly as if he were agreeing.

Then he made what for him was a very long speech:

"I am older than you, Don Buenita. I can remember the first American military occupation. I played with the marines. They were nice but they built the big roads. Then people began to move to the capital. The Americans left and gave us Trujillo, who built the capital and wanted people to move there. He wanted to teach *los campesinos* to wear shoes and to work for his benefit. Everyone had to pay taxes to Trujillo, and no one could oppose him unless they were ready to go to prison or die. He owned the country but he forgot *los campesinos.* He built schools and hospitals and electrical plants for the capital and the cities and brought running water from the mountains. The *campesinos* began to leave the countryside in search of a less harsh life. No one will convince me that they actually obtained an easy life, and even if they had, to me a soft life can't replace producing something real, like growing coffee, *platanos, maíz* (corn), and yucas and taking care of the animals that help us. Yes, it is a very wretched life here, but I am proud of a life of hard work."

"Don María, thank you for the coffee," Don Buenita nodded. "I respect and appreciate you very much, but we never will agree."

My mother appeared just when Don Buenita was about to leave. With a small, sweet smile, she said that Holanda had read Papalo's letter to her.

"He has joined the army."

She delivered the message proudly, but María grew angrier. Out of respect for the presence of Buenita, he directed his rage toward the absent Papalo.

"Look, Don Buenita," María said, "Papalo, like many others who join the army, will lose his freedom. He will not be able to do anything without the approval of his superior; he can't come home without permission. I don't care about all this as much as I worry about him becoming *un parrandero* (a reveler), *un alcohólico* (an alcoholic) *y peor un abusador del poder* (and worst, an abuser of power)."

After Buenita left, the only sound was an ominous stirring from the mango, avocado, and palm trees tossed by a strong afternoon breeze as if a hurricane might be approaching. My mother stood in the kitchen giving my father a hard look.

I knew that hearing him talk about the possibility that one of her sons would ever become a reveler, an alcoholic, and an abuser distressed her deeply. She was raising her children to be respectful human beings—to be good and to do good. She taught all of us to be kind, to be respectful, and to never harm anyone. I knew that if I failed to live up to her values, it would constitute an unforgivable betrayal of her and my family.

But María sounded so utterly pessimistic, so sure of a bad outcome for Papalo, that I thought he might be right. This was as distressing to me as the possibility I would end up in hell for my childish misdeeds.

Full of fears, I began to doubt whether leaving the campo was best for all of us. I wished both of my parents could be right. Why does it have to be one or the other? Why could it not be both? Some of us could go. Some of us could stay. Couldn't they agree on that? On my mother's side, there was pride, being the master of your own destiny, chasing a dream, optimism, and breaking away from current circumstance; on María's, fatalism, the land, our way of life that was the way of our ancestors— planting, cultivating, and harvesting your food—and perhaps the scar left on his soul by Trujillo.

My father always said you are supposed to die where you were born; my mother said you know where you were born but you don't know where you are going to die. My mother was not ready to accept life as it was—not without fighting to change it. My father was happy with his circumstances.

He was headstrong. He wanted everyone to see things as he did. But my mother was even more headstrong.

Not even an innocent young boy like me, innocent as a dove, could escape being scarred by seeing so many cousins, brothers and sisters, uncles, and friends move away while I waited for my turn, the turn my mother had promised me.

As a pragmatic woman, my mother didn't accept the idea of emotional scars. She would say, "*Déjame ver tu cicatriz*"—Let me see your scar. I can hear her sweet, gentle voice undulating in the air over and over to be sure I heard her with both my ears.

She bet on education and helping us to escape from the farm. She wanted all of us to go to school, which for her meant learning how to write, to read, and to be a good person. To my mother, getting an education meant opening up opportunities, from the military, which required an eighth-grade education, to jobs that would ensure a life beyond a peasant's existence.

When my grandmother and my mother were growing up, parents, particularly in the countryside, were not expected to send their children to school. There often were no schools to send them to. My mother was the first in her family who had a school within reach (six kilometers away), one with three grades. But her parents didn't send her to it.

She often said, "My mother didn't know how to write and read, and I don't either."

One time, it occurred to me to ask her why not.

"There was no school here at first and, anyway, during those days girls were not expected to go to school," she said. "And my mother didn't see that school was important."

"Why not?" I asked again.

"Ever since I was a young girl, I was expected to help my mother with the household chores. Just as I do now, I carried water from the river to the bohio and helped with cooking, sewing, washing clothes, and grinding coffee."

"Your father didn't grind the coffee and make his coffee like María?" I asked. This was a new idea.

"Men didn't cook"

"María does."

"He only knows how to make coffee, and only because I refuse to get up every morning to make his coffee. I have enough to do on the farm and with the children. I don't want that kind of life for my sons and daughters."

She didn't need to say it again: Education is the gateway out of the hamlet and to a better life than she had known. She didn't need to say it again, but she did. Often.

The education she'd set her sights on for us was limited to the fundamentals, which in her view was enough to get us out of the hamlet and succeed in the capital. She could never have imagined the end of the path she set me on.

As I matured, I became more conflicted about the military. My sister Luz's husband was a colonel in the Dominican navy and he helped two of my brothers and my cousins join the ranks. They would all say that it changed their lives for the better.

But by the time I was in seventh grade, my beloved teacher, Juan Ramos, had instilled in my mind the idea that the Dominican military's role was to serve the personal and political interest of President Balaguer more than to serve the country. The only time that he would speak with anger was when he wanted to impress on us that El Jefe, as he called Trujillo, had demanded 100 percent personal loyalty from the military and that Balaguer was like Trujillo.

I learned that my teacher's father had been killed by Trujillo's military. I began to doubt what my brother-in-law told me regarding the military as a way to protect the country from communism and, specifically, from Fidel Castro.

I already knew I didn't want to follow Papalo's path. I would rather be like Arsenio, who never joined the army but was doing well. Every time he visited, he kept pushing me to do well in school as if he knew that was the best way out of the hamlet.

The struggle in my *bohio* continued. Although my father would soften his stance when Papalo sent money to help support the farm, he never conceded that it was a good choice to leave. In the end, my mother's unwavering tenacity would prevail.

Today, I am self-aware. I can describe the emotional and psychological impact of watching my family members leave home one by one. And, given the education my mother ensured for me, I can read words of wisdom that would both comfort her and make her proud that her son could access such resources.

"Cuando ya no somos capaces de cambiar una situación, tenemos el desafío de cambiarnos a nosotros mismos."

Viktor E. Frankl

Reflect and Imagine Activity

Family matters

Families play a critical role in the education of their children, and collaboration between teachers and families is a key to increasing the likelihood of students' achievement. It is not an easy task to establish good relationships with families from challenging circumstances like mine, but it is not impossible to do so. It requires learning a bit about the culture, education level, socioeconomic conditions, and the capacity of the family to meet the school's expectations, such as helping the child with homework and the ability to read the communications from school to the home.

Getting to know your students' families also requires commitment from the school administration. For example, does the administration provide the necessary support to conduct a home visit to a family like mine? Does the administration limit the number of students like me in any one classroom?

Consider the variations among the families of your ELL students. Consider that most immigrant families have sought new lives because they are ambitious for their children. How can the teacher tap into that ambition to assist the child's learning? But consider also that their new world often finds families unfamiliar with our school cultures and often unable to provide guidance in schoolwork. Nonetheless, the family's values can reinforce behavior that is conducive to achievement.

Consider what you have learned about my family that may help you understand my needs as a student. What assumptions do you have about my family's strengths and weaknesses? The strengths of my family, for example, include both my parents respecting teachers and my mother's strong desire for me to get a good education. Weaknesses might include lack of educational resources at home to help me with lessons or a failure to provide a role model for reading.

My younger self was taught to be obedient above all; to respect my parents, elders, and teachers; and not to contradict them by asking questions. How might this translate into my behavior in a classroom? Is this entirely beneficial? For instance, might this respectfulness work against the freedom to question that our culture takes for granted? Might these qualities appear to you to be docility or passivity? Might they mask difficulties with learning, with school, or at home?

Young Bolgen (the student described in chapter 1) attends school every day, is well behaved, and has made significant progress in numeracy and literacy but is still far behind most peers. As you approach the summer school break, you are concerned he may suffer setbacks due to the summer learning loss. What can you and the school do to mitigate the summer learning loss? What can the family do? What can young Bolgen do? What can a neighborhood do?

You have learned a lot about me and my family, so how can you share what you know with his next teacher to help jumpstart his year?

Imagine that you *don't* have any information about my family. What assumptions and questions come to your mind about my family?

I recognize that most teachers understand that getting to know their students' families requires time, resources, and a certain skill set that includes appreciation and understanding for culture and language that are different from that of the teacher. Although no teacher can begin to know about every family's culture in our extraordinarily diverse country, genuine curiosity and interest can go a long way.

The following are some resources that might strengthen your ability to connect with families that are not defined as "mainstream" but who are nevertheless striving to do the best they can, as mine did, although their efforts may not be visible to the teacher.

Howard, K. (2020). *Stop talking about wellbeing: A pragmatic approach to teacher workload.* John Catt Educational.

Kat Howard addresses how teachers can take ownership of their workload to address their own well-being so that they can be more effective and achieve their primary goal: to teach children and young people. You cannot teach a child well whom you don't know well. One of the primary benefits of teachers getting to know their students and their families is that it helps them to understand what sparks the students' (and families') motivations and desires. However, getting to know your students and their families is often not easy, particularly when the families come from a variety of cultural, social, and economic backgrounds and speak different languages. In my experience, teacher workload often gets in the way of both teachers' well-being and that of their students. But those barriers could be broken if the teachers receive sufficient support from school leaders to be responsive to their own and their students' well-being. Howard's book offers a pragmatic approach to handling teacher workload and well-being.

Gonzalez, N. E., Moll, L., & Amanti, C. (Eds.). (2005). *Funds of knowledge: Theorizing practices in households and classrooms.* Lawrence Erlbaum Associates.

This book will help you discover the "funds of knowledge" that students like young Bolgen might bring to the classroom and, most significantly, how you can bring these skills right into the curriculum. The concepts found in this book are easier for elementary teachers to apply than for middle and high school teachers, who typically have a considerably larger number of students in their caseloads. Nevertheless, I believe these essays offer useful insights for all teachers who are working with a diverse student population. In essence, the *Funds of Knowledge* approach fosters respect, appreciation, and understanding of the experiences of students from diverse cultures, languages, and ways of knowing. It calls for teachers to learn about the resources that students like young Bolgen and his family bring to school, and to understand that these attributes may be less transparent than the traditional values, cultural norms, and knowledge that the overwhelming majority of middle- and upper-income students bring to the classroom.

Nieto. S. (2005). *Why we teach*. Teachers College Press.

This is a wonderful book for any teacher who works with a diverse student population, including but not limited to ELLs. Teachers can visualize themselves in the classrooms of the 21 teachers who talk about their experiences working with very diverse student populations. When I first read this book, I saw myself as a student in some of those classrooms. The stories provide hope for teachers who are working with the most vulnerable kids when far too many public schools tend to have punitive environments due to internal and external pressure to produce students with high standardized test scores.

Nieto, S. (2015). *Why we teach now*. Teachers College Press.

A sequel to *Why We Teach*, this book offers invigorating accounts in 23 essays by teachers who work in a range of school settings around the United States, with a focus on how public education has changed in the past two decades. If you have been teaching in the past decade, you will find these essays affirming your experiences from a turbulent time, offering good reasons why you keep teaching. One conclusion I draw from this volume is that, in the long run, successful teaching and learning for the most vulnerable children depends on being hopeful as a teacher and as an administrator.

Chapter 3

America came to us before we came to America

"Fuera Yanqui y Llevame Contigo" ("Yankee go home and take me with you")

By the time Papalo ran away from the farm, my brother Arsenio had already moved from the capital to the ultimate destination for a Dominican seeking greater opportunity: New York City. Nueva York. America. The USA. Home of the *gringo*.

The meaning of the word gringo varies, depending on who is using it. When my father said, *"cuando llegaron los gringos,"* he meant, "when the Americans arrived"—by which he meant the American marines. They had come in 1916 to impose order at a chaotic time in my country's life. They stayed eight years.

Why is it important that America came to us before we came to America? Because America set the stage for our belief that opportunities were abundant in its land of plenty.

The Dominican Republic and the US have had a complicated relationship for almost two centuries, one that directly shaped my life. Through my father, I can reach back to my family's first contact with the idea of America, the land, as it turned out, of our destiny.

In 1918, when my father was 12 years old and the country was occupied by the US, the central government passed compulsory education legislation intended to cover all children aged seven to 14. Although the legislation was a good first step, neither the American government, which effectively ruled the island at the time, nor the Dominican government built enough schools or prepared enough teachers to serve the majority of students, particularly those living in rural areas. This deficit continued through my own childhood half a century later, and to a certain degree it is still so today, particularly in the most impoverished areas of the country.

The American military forces were gone by 1924, but for my father their influence was already changing the reality of everyday life in the countryside. His memory of the gringos stayed as vivid and clear as the sun rising in a cloudless Caribbean sky.

Nothing about their presence was more consequential in his mind than the paved roads the gringos built, which made it practical for people and goods to move between the *campos* and the cities. This resulted in the mass exodus of *campesinos* to Santo Domingo, the capital, and ultimately to the US. It left my father stuck forever in internal and external conflict between the virtues of life in the countryside and life in the city.

His tales of the gringos were amusing, most of all when he tried to tell us how gringos sounded when they the spoke: "*pspspspspsps*." He liked to pretend that he could speak English and he sounded so funny to me that I would ask him to tell me about his childhood experience *con Americanos*.

He would recount, "*Los Marinos* would come by on packhorses looking for *los gavilleros* (gunmen), and they were friendly to us because we didn't have anything to hide. We were not part of the *gavilleros* who were fighting to end the occupation."

María remembered an occasion when his mother offered the *marinos* her *sancocho* (stew), but they politely declined and kept going with huge rifles, looking everywhere for *los gavilleros*.

When the marines returned in 1965 for a brief occupation—at a time of political upheaval the US was afraid might lead to a communist takeover—a slogan appeared scrawled on walls around the capital: *Yankee go home and take me with you!*

They say home is where the heart is. But, for a large proportion of the world's population, home is where work is, where food is, and where safety is.

Before I was born, Arsenio, who was my third oldest sibling, had moved to Santo Domingo to live with my uncle, hoping to go to school there. Instead, he went to work at my uncle's store.

Arsenio was the first in my family to realize that no matter how hard he worked it would not be possible for him to help improve our situation back in our hamlet, or even in the capital. He was always a hard worker and maybe he would have done well for himself in the capital, but he was not interested in improving his own condition without improving the condition of his immediate and extended family.

If home *is* where the heart is, then my brother Arsenio's heart must have broken when in 1968, at 23 years old, he obtained a tourist visa to enter in the United States and left the island for New York City to make an opportunity for the rest of us to follow.

I carry deep and intense feelings in my soul that began the day we learned that my brother was leaving for New York. At that moment on a late afternoon when we heard the news, my mother began to pray. At night her prayers became longer than usual, with the sole focus on her son's safe journey and then his safety in the new land. In her prayer she asked repeatedly of *La Santima Virgen de la Altagracia*, the country's official patron saint and protector of the heart of Dominicans, and to *el gran Dios*, to bless her precious son and to protect him from all evils and from the evil eye.

Two weeks later the news came that Arsenio had arrived safely to *Nueva York* and he was working and living with a family from Bonao who cared about his well-being.

As it turned out, if Arsenio's heart broke, it soon mended. He met his future wife, Ydalia, in his new home, where she too had come from the island to make an opportunity for her family. They married, raised three children, and remain happily married to this day.

Arsenio & Ydalia as a young couple

This was a time when the United States opened its gates to immigration, wanting to encourage the belief that this was the land of opportunity, democracy, and freedom where all could strive.

My brother's journey had an immediate impact on our lives. The purpose of moving to a strange place was for the sake of the family. He never failed to send us $10–$20 a month, which made a huge difference to us.

Immediately, it meant enough food on the table and, more important to me, the ability to buy a notebook, a pencil, and the required school uniform—a pair of khaki brown pants and a khaki brown shirt. No shoes were necessary, *gracias a Dios*. That was one less obstacle to overcome to go to school to get a little formal education. I was eight years old.

But his greatest gift to me was setting high expectations and providing the encouragement I needed to succeed in school and in life—he was a true role model and hero for me. Although Arsenio's formal schooling didn't go beyond the sixth grade, his sacrifices allowed me to beat the same odds he faced. He worked as a superintendent in a building in Greenwich Village, and he did more than help me succeed in school and in life. He gave me hope. My dream to get a good education would never dry up as long as the sea exists and the day and the night are still with us.

When I was little, aside from my father's stories, just about everything I knew about America came from baseball, which was the other lasting change the American marines made to life on the island. They brought the game with them and left it with us to become really good at. My first idea of America was of a faraway land where all the very best baseball players go. I learned this from my brothers and the other older boys in the hamlet. Every boy I knew wanted to play in America.

Another of my early impressions of America came from the taste of powdered milk.

When I was born, the world was divided between competing superpowers, the US and the Soviet Union. Both had their eyes on the Dominican Republic. The United States was determined to prevent the Dominican Republic from becoming another Cuba.

After the US marines left the island for the second time, the America government began to send food, medical supplies, and other types of aid to ensure stability and establish a better life for Dominicans. In the 1960s, the US sent more foreign aid per capita to us than any other nation except South Vietnam.

My first day at school, I tasted the effect of this American aid. I've forgotten everything about that day except my first school meal.

Just before we were dismissed, I was served a US wheat grain meal made with US powdered milk, Dominican sugar, cinnamon, and lemon flavor from the leaves on the tree outside the three-room schoolhouse. This dish was rich, sweet, and creamy like the special Dominican sweet bean dish my mother made every Easter. She used goat milk in hers, but it was not as tasty as the powdered milk from the faraway US. I walked home with a happy belly. A seed had been planted—I began to be aware of America as a land of plenty.

Although "Yankee go home and take us with you!" was not an entirely ironic sentiment by the time the marines left the island again, it didn't happen that way—they didn't take us with them. Instead, Dominicans had to follow them, many risking their lives to pursue the American dream.

The most fortunate, like my brother, arrived by air. But many crossed the 80 miles to Puerto Rico by sea—across *el mar de los muertos* (the sea of the dead) as the treacherous strait was known for the many who died in the crossing—to reach the closest US territory.

Between 1966 and 1976, more than one million Dominicans arrived in the United States to pursue dreams of a better life they couldn't realize at home.

My most direct contact with the dream of a better life in America came from the small funds Arsenio continued to send my parents each month. Beyond meeting our immediate needs, they used the money to put a cement floor in our *bohio* and then a metal roof, huge improvements over the dirt floor and leaking palm leaf roof I'd known all my life.

But my most vivid memory of the impact of the wealth Arsenio had found in America was when he paid for my father to get dentures. Ever since I could remember, my father didn't have any teeth—not because he was so old but because we didn't have the resources for dental care. Before, his face had been sad and wrinkled, but when he got his dentures he looked younger and happier. He was transformed. I began to dream about coming to America.

A few years later, in December, during the rainy season, Arsenio's wife Ydalia came to visit us in the hamlet. And she brought something miraculous—a tape recorder. I didn't know that such a thing existed. We gathered around in a circle looking at a small black, flat, rectangular object. She pressed a button and Arsenio's voice came out. He sent his warmest greetings as if he knew how much we missed him and wanted to cheer us. When we heard his voice, the small room in our home lit up with our smiles. Even María couldn't hide the joy of hearing his son's voice.

It was a magical moment for me. It left me wondering, how could this be possible? To speak to us from so far away? I felt that he was physically present in our circle. America must be a very special place.

When I heard that the Americans had landed on the moon, I began to think of Americans as crazy smart. To me, the moon landing made Americans as powerful as the moon itself. I knew the constancy of the sun, but the moon was mythical with its ever-changing shape and size and location in the sky.

Now I saw the Americans as mythical too. How are they able to make cars, radios, airplanes, ships, and submarines that travel under the ocean? Now I was experiencing a miracle, listening to my brother speak to me via a tape.

America made this possible. I suddenly wanted to be with Arsenio in America. But I thought it would be as difficult to join my brother in America as it would be for me to travel to the moon.

A year later, Arsenio came home. He had an appointment to go to the United States Consulate to be interviewed to qualify for a "green card," permanent resident status in the US. He said his dream was to bring my mother and the rest of us to New York.

There was a time when my mother saw Santo Domingo as the destination for all her children. But after the brief US invasion of 1965, Arsenio, like many other Dominicans, realized there was a more promising destination. At that time in New York City, even *campesinos* like me and my family members could find jobs in garment factories and restaurants, and as janitors, nannies, doormen, porters, and hospital workers.

Arsenio said that you could earn more in a week in New York City than you could in a month in the Dominican capital. He was able to support my parents much better from New York City than when he was in Santo Domingo. He wasn't alone. According to some estimates, by 1990, one of every 10 Dominicans in the US was living in New York City.

I was fascinated when Arsenio described skyscrapers. I was almost disbelieving when he described the Empire State Building. And when he said, "I work en un edificio grande"—he was a "super"—I wondered what that meant. He operated an elevator, took care of the boiler, and kept the building clean.

Elevator? Boiler? These and so many other words that Arsenio was using to describe his experience and New York City were completely foreign to me. The industrial revolution had not arrived in our hamlet. There were cars on the highway, but we had no boilers. He'd come a long way from the farm!

"My dream is that one day I will bring all of you to New York City, the capital of the world, with opportunities for work," he said. "For a young boy like you, Chichilo, there are a lot of opportunities to go to school, study hard, and become a professional."

It felt good that Arsenio and my mother were setting expectations for me even if I didn't fully understand it all. They wanted me to do well in school and to stay in school longer than my siblings. The boys had all left school to work before completing the eighth grade. I didn't know anyone from the hamlet who had finished high school. I found school exciting— and easier than work on the farm.

Arsenio's new life offered him and his family more than we had. But he also made it clear that his life was not easy, with long hours of work and the challenges of adapting to a foreign country, a different culture, and a different language. The worst, he said, was the weather. He told us about the snow, the ice on the street, rivers covered by ice, and the days that passed without ever seeing the sun, the sky covered in the gray of winter.

Arsenio wanted me to understand that despite a lot of opportunity in New York, the city is not a paradise. I had been forming a picture of a land of plenty, where life was always easier.

Just before Christmas in 1973, hope became a light that shone on a new path for my mother and my siblings. A letter arrived from Arsenio containing $25 and instructions for obtaining copies of notarized birth certificates for her and my brother Digno.

Arsenio would need these to file a petition to start the two-year immigration process for them to obtain alien registration cards that would allow them to immigrate to the US. Digno, the lucky boy, was chosen because he was 18 years old, enough under the 21-year-old threshold that would still allow my mother to petition for him to accompany her as a dependent family member. In addition, since he was of working age, both he and

Octavia could demonstrate the ability to support themselves in America without being dependent on government assistance.

Arsenio secured affidavits verifying that each would have immediate employment. Digno would be a fast-food cook at a Spanish restaurant on the corner of Orchard and Stanton Streets, and Octavia would cook and clean dishes at a Puerto Rican cuchifrito, a small fried food restaurant, on Avenue C in the neighborhood where she would be living.

Settling in New York would pave the way for my mother to petition for me, my father, and my sister Patricia to follow them.

Two years later, Octavia made the trip to Santo Domingo, obtained the necessary papers from the consulate, and started making plans to leave the hamlet.

The evening she came home with her papers, my parents had a pleasant conversation. My father had always been against any of us moving away. He saw it as a loss, with nothing to gain. This time he seemed neutral; I couldn't tell whether he was in favor of or against my mother moving away.

I remember asking, "Who is going to cook for my father and me?" By now, all my siblings had left the hamlet for the capital and America. With my mother gone, it would be just María and me. There was silence. And I knew better than to push for an answer.

She would return to Santo Domingo the following Friday to board a flight on Dominicana Airlines to New York City with Digno and Arsenio. I would have four more days with my mother. I would go to Santo Domingo to see my brothers and sisters who lived there and take my mother to the airport with them. It hadn't occurred to me that my father would not be going with us. But he did not. I shouldn't have been surprised.

The evening ended with tears, laughter, and prayers. We did very little to get ready because my mother wouldn't take any clothing other than what she was wearing. She gave the little clothing she had to our most needy friends. Arsenio had brought her a nice dress to wear on her visit to the American Consulate and then on the trip to New York City. He always said that in New York, the clothes and food were much less expensive than in the Dominican Republic.

I was happy for my mother but crushed to be left behind. Once Octavia was settled in the United States, she could begin the two-year process of obtaining visas for my father, Patricia, and me through the immigration law that allowed for reunification of immediate family. It was painful but I accepted it. My mother had taught me well how to face adversity.

We had two days in the capital before she would say goodbye. Arsenio told me this: "All you have to do is to concentrate on your education. Go to school every day and make every effort to learn. Respect *el Maestro*, the teacher. When you get to America you will be young enough to achieve a good education. You will have more opportunity than any of us had. I only wish that I could have been as fortunate."

He gave me five dollars, which was a lot of money for a boy from the country. Any work that I did and every penny that I earned was to help support the family. In my family you didn't own anything until you were old enough to be out of the house. My father owned everything that we had. So, I kept the five dollars a secret. But I came to realize that the real gift my brother had given me was the encouragement he delivered with caring and sincere love.

At the airport, Octavia gave me a long hug and told me to be *fuerte*, strong. I saw her walk toward the plane with Arsenio and Digno. I wanted her to look back. But she didn't. My eyes had never been so focused, I saw her taking every slow step in the passenger line, showing her papers and answering questions to the Dominican authority, the airline authority, and the immigration authority as if she were the most worldly of travelers. Then, she disappeared from my sight.

We moved to a place where we could see the plane on the ground. I focused my eyes on the airplane ladder until I saw my mother. She walked straight into the airplane without looking back.

Reflect and Imagine Activity

Reading, writing, and other literacies
Perhaps you meet one or more newly arrived immigrant students on the first day of a new school year in your classroom or elsewhere in your school community. The language skills, cultural backgrounds, motivations,

and level of formal education they bring from their native countries are important to understand as a teacher and leader charged with educating students with backgrounds like mine.

It is hard to teach a child whose background you do not know well. The backgrounds of most ELL students are, more often than not, challenging to dissect, and certainly it is not possible to do so with a single assessment tool.

Take, for example, my experience growing up in the hamlet surrounded by widespread illiteracy and poverty, both of which are associated with poor education outcomes. My circumstances prior to my arrival in the US might suggest to most people, including some well-intentioned educators, that my siblings and I wouldn't have received a good start in gaining literacy in our home or in our hamlet.

Although that might seem to be a reasonable assumption, it does not adequately consider the new knowledge about literacy and how we acquire it both inside and outside the classroom. My mother and my family actually provided me with a rich amount of exposure to activities that contributed to my literacy development and more significantly to my love of learning for the sake of it.

For instance, my mother recited the daily prayer every evening. She was wonderful with *dichos* (sayings). Two of my favorites were *Te conozco, bacalao, aunque vengas disfrazao* (I will know you even if you are disguised) and *hacerse el chivo loco* (to become the crazy goat; meaning to play dumb, to be irresponsible). I was never allowed to get away with playing the "crazy goat." My mother taught me to be responsible as a student and as a person. My mother also was extraordinarily good at reciting *decimas Dominicana*, a form of folkloric poetry. Hence, even though she didn't know how to read or write, she introduced me to a special experience of words, which helped when I started to become literate—as I did in my first years of school in the hamlet. By this time in my story, I knew my letters and was reading children's stories in school.

If the ELL teacher in America knew this, he or she could help bridge young Bolgen's background to the classroom, building on pre-literate language strengths to foster academic literacy in reading, writing, and beyond.

A challenge for teachers and other educators—of both ELL students and native speakers—is to go beyond the way literacy is defined for school success. Consider the simplicity of how literacy—which comes from the Latin word for *letter*—has been defined for most of history: the ability to read and write.

In his 1989 classic, *Lives on the Boundary*, the educator and author Mike Ross gives this thumbnail history of how the concept of functional literacy has evolved.

In the 1930s 'functional literacy' was defined by the Civilian Conservation Corps as a state of having three or more years of schooling; during World War II the army set the fourth grade as a standard; in 1947 the Census Bureau defined functional illiterates as those having fewer than five years of schooling; in 1952 the bureau raised the criterion to the sixth grade; by 1960 the Office of Education was setting the eighth grade as a benchmark; and by the late 1970s some authorities were suggesting that completion of high school should be the defining criterion for functional literacy. (p. 6)

Now, half a century later, teachers and educators work with their students in a world that has seen even more significant change in the meaning of literacy, including the expansion of the term to include multiple literacies and the ways literacy is assessed. Our definitions of literacy have become more complex to reflect the changes in our world. Today, *literacy* refers to skills and knowledge beyond reading and writing. Examples include digital literacy, media literacy, and cultural literacy among others. These represent necessary skills in today's world that were not relevant just a few decades ago. Consider how much easier your job would have been when literacy was defined more simply—as just reading and writing— than today with the complexity of multiple literacies. And consider that students like Bolgen bring unique skills and knowledge that you can blend into their literacies in your classroom.

Now, consider the following:

Going beyond the definition of literacy as reading and writing, what kind of literacies do students, like young Bolgen, from diverse languages, cultures, economic status, and religions bring to the school and the classrooms? How can you use these skills to help him become literate in English as defined by the ability to read and write at grade level? Assume he came to your fifth-grade class directly from the Dominican Republic.

In addition to the school, what organizations and institutions exist in your neighborhood and community that can support young Bolgen's literacy development?

Should students coming from backgrounds similar to young Bolgen's have to wait until they master literacy and numeracy skills before they can be exposed to higher level work involving critical thinking and "deep learning"?

Imagine

You have discovered that even though young Bolgen's literacy skills in English are far below the fifth-grade level, you see that he is far ahead of his peers in math. You believe that in the next school year he should be placed in the advanced math class. The math teacher heard that you are recommending young Bolgen for his class and tells you that it would not be a good idea because young Bolgen does not know "much English." He is concerned that although Bolgen scored 90 in the district placement math test, he just barely passed the literacy test. And he repeats that Bolgen's poor English skills will get in the way.

You sense that the math teacher is not comfortable teaching kids like Bolgen. In fact, you later find that he went to the school principal and argued to overrule your recommendation—and the principal did so. What would you do to continue to advocate for vulnerable students like Bolgen? Would there be consequences? After this experience, would you agree with Sonia Nieto, who writes: "I have learned that literacy is not just teaching the mechanics of reading or imparting information to students; rather it is always either advocacy for or against the students who we teach."

References

Nieto, S. (2018). *Languages, culture, and teaching: Critical perspectives.* Routledge.

Ross, M. (1989). *Lives on the boundary: A moving account of the struggles and achievements of America's educationally underprepared.* Penguin.

Chapter 4

Waiting, hoping, and radio school

"We all ask that question, 'What is home?' It's like asking 'What is love?' It changes, it's complex."

Richard Blanco

After the long car ride from the capital and the long walk to the hamlet from the paved road, I got home when the night was just turning dark. My father was already in bed.

I entered the bedroom quietly. It was darker than the outside—pitch dark. The only sound was the chirping of crickets.

As I stood in front of my bed, I silently said a version of the rosary to fill the void left by not hearing the prayers my mother said each night of my life.

To my surprise, María said, "Now it is just the two of us here."

I took it as an invitation to talk.

I started to tell him about Octavia's departure from the airport. "I saw Octavia getting into the plane and she didn't seem scared at all."

He said, "Stop talking. I want to go to sleep."

I obeyed. I began to realize how much I was now on my own. I could not expect to get from my father what Octavia had given me every day. I was overwhelmed by the physical absence of my mother, and yet she was present.

I lay down on the bed, and even though my father was there sleeping soundlessly as always, and the sound of the mosquitos was the same, and it was as dark as always, I felt I was in a different home. A home without heartfelt love. I was awake most of the night with thoughts of Octavia walking into the airplane blocking out any other thoughts. It was as if that picture was glued to me, never to leave my mind.

I worried about the new world Octavia was facing without me. I know she is strong and confident, but how is she going to adapt to life in New York City? She did not read or write and only spoke Spanish. How will she talk to Americans? She knows how to raise cows, pigs, goats, chickens, and turkeys, and she knows how to grow *gandules* (pigeon peas), *tabaco* (tobacco), *yuca*, *maíz*, and all kinds of beans—black and red—and use all kinds of seasonings. She made the tastiest oatmeal by adding sweet chocolate, sugar, goat milk, clove, and cinnamon. But I thought that none of these skills would be very useful in New York City.

"Get up! The sun is up!" my father shouted.

I didn't respond. He shouted again. I was not happy to be awakened by his shouting, but I knew well the consequences of not jumping up—blows with his leather strap. María's annoyance with me could easily rise to anger. It was a cloudy day. I was feeling gloomy—gloomier than the weather.

"It is going to rain soon," María said. "Go to the river and get *dos calabazos de agua* (two gourds of water)."

Walking to the river with a *calabazo* in each hand, I thought of all the ways my life was changing for the worse. I would have to do everything my mother and my sisters used to do—get water, cook, clean, wash my clothes—as well as everything else my father asked me to do. But I remembered what my mother and brother said and I pushed away my negative thoughts. I repeated several times to myself that this situation would not last forever. I have to do what my mother and brother told me to do: *"Concentrate on doing well in school and by doing so you will overcome any adversity."*

I had missed more than a week of school and I couldn't wait to get back. But I was afraid that when I got home with the water my father would tell me that there was too much to be done and I couldn't go to school.

By the time I returned, it was thundering and pouring rain. My father called to me to go to the yucca field to pull up *dos yuca*. I wanted to say it is raining too hard for me to go outside, but I kept my mouth shut. I took a machete and walked as fast as I could to the yucca field. The weather was scaring me. But because the soil was wet it was fairly easy for me to pull the yuccas. The first plant I pulled had four tubers.

I peeled and cut up the yucca and I boiled it without being asked. I had watched my mother cook yucca thousands of times, so I was ready. I cooked it just like she did, adding cilantro five minutes before it was done. In the end she would sauté a little onion and pour it on top. I did exactly the same, except for one thing: I forgot to add salt.

María let me know the moment he took the first bite. *"Con un pique,"* he said, irritated. *"No tiene sal. Dame la sal"*—It does not have salt. Give me the salt.

Without another word he ate the first dish I ever cooked.

When we finished eating, the thunder stopped and the rain slowed. I attempted to tell my father what Arsenio had told me about education.

"María, Arsenio told me that to progress you must have a good education."

He responded with silence.

I said, "From now on I will not miss a single day of school."

He replied, *"Sí, muchacho, vete."*—Get out, spoiled boy.

That was better than I expected.

The sun came out strong and I was still fearful that my father would tell me there were more things to be done. There was only one thing that I wanted to do, which was to go to school.

I wasted no time. I began to read and do my school assignment on science. It was about elements: *What are the first four elements? How are elements named? What is a natural element? What is a physical element? How many elements do we have?* I did my best, but I was not able to complete the assignment because I'd missed the lesson on Radio Santa María.

In my hamlet, the school only offered first through sixth grade to students who came from a handful of hamlets—Angostura, Boca de Cabía, Boca de Caonao, and El Ranchito de los Peralta. But my teacher, Juan Ramos, who taught fifth and sixth grade, offered instruction for grades seven and eight to those of us who were fortunate enough to reach that level. His instruction was coordinated with *La Escuela Radiofonicas Santa María*— radio school. The lessons by radio were delivered four nights a week at 7 p.m. and in-person class attendance was expected five days a week from 2 to 5 p.m.

Today, we call this blended learning. We may think of it as an innovation, but in the Dominican Republic when I was a child, it was simply a necessity.

I might miss school due to obligations at home as well as heavy rains that could make the roads impassable. My teacher understood that my obligations were a matter of putting food on the table. He knew my mother and father well and all my siblings. María was always generous with my teacher; we shared our yuccas and plantains with his family.

My teacher understood the conflicting and competing interest that the majority of his students were facing: survival versus education. He was on my side and he knew that now that my mother was gone I would be at risk of dropping out due to the demands of work at home and the lack of support and encouragement from my father.

At 12:30 the first afternoon I was home from the capital, I ran barefoot to school. Along the way I saw Tortola, a friend of my mother, with her daughter, each carrying two huge *calabazos*, one on the head and the other in hand.

They wanted to talk to me and shouted, "Why are you running? Octavia left on the plane?"

I shouted back, "Sí" and kept running. I needed to get to school early to speak with my teacher. When I arrived, he was there alone getting ready to receive his students.

I said, "Maestro, can I speak with you?"

In my country, as well as in many Spanish-speaking countries, students typically do not use the teacher's name. The title "Maestro" signifies a highly respected role and a position of status, particularly in my hamlet. (I was to learn that in the US, "Teacher" is not an appropriate form of address.) He was the only person I'd ever met who spoke educated Spanish.

"Of course," he said with a comforting smile. "But first tell me about your mother's trip to New York."

I was no longer able to hold back all my sadness and emotion, and I broke down in tears.

"She flew away to New York. And you know I am alone with my father, who is likely to stop me from coming to school as he did with my brothers."

He gave me a strong hug and said, "Don't worry I will talk to Don María. I will tell him that you need to come to school because you are not going to stay here. This is a different time than when he grew up. I will change his mind."

Mr. Ramos was a soft-spoken older man who had only one thing in common with my father—they were both bald. Maestro explained that when my father was growing up, although the school offered classes up to third grade, the majority of children didn't attend. María didn't go to school; his parents and his grandparents didn't go to school.

I thanked him and then explained that I hadn't finished the assignment and needed help with it.

He understood. "I know that you were preoccupied with your mother's trip. I will go over the assignment today. Just pay attention and I won't call on you to answer any questions."

I was relieved and happy. I joined my classmates gathered under the mango and palm trees.

We were called in to class. Everyone was happy to be there. Our school was extremely overcrowded. Four of us squashed together on old benches that had been designed to accommodate three at most. We were crushed for the majority of the class, which was only relieved when the teacher called one of us to come to the blackboard.

There were about 100 students in my teacher's four grades, far too many for one teacher to teach at four different levels. Yet, I was fortunate. At least I had a school with a great teacher. Although he didn't have any formal education beyond high school, he was more qualified than the other teachers who had only an eighth-grade education. He taught us to think critically, to read, to write, and to do math; above all, he taught us the love of learning, and to be good human beings and to serve others. He was caring, loving, and gentle, and we loved and admired him. He understood the true meaning of the word *education*—from Latin, for *nourish, to bring up*—and he used his humanity in the service of teaching and learning. He was gifted. I wanted to be just like him.

That afternoon, when he ended the class, he came to my bench and said, "I hope you are feeling better."

"*Sí, Maestro, me siento mucho major.*"

He said, "I hope to see you tomorrow and I am going to talk with Don María soon."

"Gracias."

My cousin Oscar, who was in my class, was waiting outside to give me a ride home on his donkey. The donkey appeared to be annoyed with me, maybe because he'd been waiting too long. He wouldn't let me get close and he walked away when Oscar tried to hold him still. It took several attempts before I successfully jumped on. The *aparejo* (saddle cloth) was too small for both of us to fit, even though we were skinny boys, so carrying me on his bare back was probably also aggravating to the donkey.

But despite all this, while Oscar and I talked mostly about my mother and my likely departure to New York someday, the donkey trotted at a good pace and before I knew it, I was in front of my *bohio*.

I was thinking of everything that was wonderful about my mother—her love, her prayers, her kindness, and, most of all, the safety and security that she provided to me—and when I entered the *bohio* I suddenly felt empty, as if all my energy and feelings had been drained from me.

But a powerful thought poured into my mind, something my mother always told me: "You are blessed because you have a school and a teacher." Her words in my memory penetrated my whole body and gave me the energy to do everything to prove her right. I was blessed because I had an opportunity to attend school and she hadn't.

I wonder how different Octavia's life could have been, and for that matter my father's life and the lives of his entire generation, if they'd had a school and a teacher. Compared to the few privileges my parents had, I had no reason ever to feel self-pity, then or now.

When the schoolhouse that offered first through third grades was built in our part of the countryside, my parents were too old to benefit. The majority of people of their generation were illiterate, not by choice but by circumstance.

Often, people from more privileged communities with access to education condescended to us as *"burros and burras,"* as ignorant and unteachable. I never took the reference personally because my mother brought me up to be confident in myself and in my intelligence. But when it was used about my mother, implying she was ignorant because she couldn't read or write, it made me angry because I knew she was a smart woman. She was wise. In her wisdom, she prepared me to handle adversity with hope.

The evening of my first day back in school, half an hour before it was time to turn on the radio to listen to my lesson, I was very hungry. That afternoon my father had cooked *un moro arroz arenque*—rice with dried salted herring. I took a bite and it was so salty that I spit it out the second that it touched my mouth. My mother was right. She told me that my father didn't know how to cook and I was not going to be able to eat the food he prepared. She had told me that Mama (my grandmother) and my aunts Martina, Chicha, and Cornelia would not let me go hungry. I ran straight up the hill to where my grandmother lived in one of the nicer *bohios*, which my uncle had built for her. There was a big plate of rice and beans with chicken fingers waiting for me.

Mama wanted to hear about Octavia before anything else. I told her that I saw Octavia get on the airplane, and I saw it take off and slowly fade away into the high blue and white sky. She smiled at me and said I should feel better because if something had gone wrong with the plane we would have known by now. I agreed. I was sorry that I had to leave her to listen to *La Escuelas Radiofonicas Santa María* and complete my school assignments. She gave me a plate of food and wished me well with my homework.

The evening's lesson was about the history of Greek civilization. It began with the same directions as always: make sure to have a pencil, pay attention, and make sure that you are sitting in a place where you can't be interrupted.

I was too hungry to concentrate and only began to absorb the lesson after I finished eating, about 15 minutes after the lesson started. Hunger will always get in the way of learning and individual progress. My Mama and my aunts made sure that I never experienced extreme suffering from hunger. But I saw too many of my fellow students and friends afflicted by hunger. Our *conuco*, our extended family, and my grandmother kept us somewhat safe from the extreme hunger that causes you to suffer all night, awake, waiting for the morning to arrive still without anything to eat. There were days when we only had one meal; most days we had two, but we rarely had three.

That changed after my mother went to New York and began sending us money. I managed to secure three meals between my Mama and aunts and our *conuco*. Octavia educated me to be resourceful.

If I had not received so many letters from my mother during those difficult years when we were separated by the huge Atlantic Ocean, I do not think I would have made it through. They never failed to bring me comfort and joy. My sister-in-law Ydalia wrote the letters for my mother.

They were all special to me, but the first letter was the most memorable. I remember reading it to María: "Querido María y Chichilo"—Dear María and Chichilo. As I read the first line to María, my eyes became wet as I experienced joy and relief pouring out through my tears. The letter was two pages and $30 was enclosed for María and $10 for me. My family in New York recognized that I would be fending for myself much of the time while living alone with María. The letter said that all was well. Octavia and Digno had found work immediately and were living in an apartment with Ydalia's mother and her two sisters.

Octavia and me in her NYC apartment 2006

Subsequent letters told of her emerging life in this foreign place. She talked about the strangeness of the city, the cold and snow. But she never complained about anything.

Octavia's essential skills were useful for her adjustment to life there. She knew how to clean, she knew how to cook, and she was gifted at taking care of children. Her first job was in a small Puerto Rican restaurant not far from where she lived; her second job was as a nanny. She loved every child as her own and they returned the same unconditional love. Kids, young and older, loved her cooking; everyone knew when she was cooking because of the way she mixed the spices and fresh herbs, releasing pleasant aromas and thrilling flavors in the food.

Before she left the island, my mother told me, "My son, we are separated by the sea but not for too long of a time." She repeated this in her letters.

And then, suddenly, I was saying goodbye to my friends and my hamlet as I got ready to join my mother in New York. Unexpectedly, my father was coming with me.

Reflect and Imagine Activity

Old ways in a new world

When I describe my elementary and middle school experiences, some might conclude that I was poorly educated during my early years. Even though that might be a fair assumption based on US standards, I would disagree. Although my teacher had no formal pedagogical training, I always knew he was caring, loving, and committed to his students. Even in the US, when you are teaching kids like me, you may find yourself in a situation where you don't have the tools, the texts, or the adequate preparation to fully meet the needs of your students. But, like my *maestro*, teachers in the US and elsewhere in the world do manage to help their students against extraordinary odds.

My experience in the three-room schoolhouse gave me some insight into how important it is for teachers to have the freedom to respond to the individual needs of their students. For example, my teacher would have a class of 35 students cramped in a small space with no educational materials and only a beat-up blackboard and chalk. Out of necessity, his sole instructional method was direct instruction, which is often criticized in the US as ineffective in that it doesn't engage the students. However, if you are trying to meet the individual instructional needs of kids at multiple grade levels, you must use the most appropriate method to fit the situation.

In seventh and eighth grade, I was introduced to what currently is called blended learning, where I received two hours of direct instruction and one hour via radio. As Katie Novak and Caitlin Tucker wrote in *UDL and Blended Learning* (2021):

It is important to note that implementing UDL and blended learning does not mean that there is not direct instruction... Direct instruction will always have a place in education…To support the direct instruction, teachers provide students with choices to help support their learning and offer multiple ways to dive deeper into the information covered through direct instruction, for example by giving a student the option to read a chapter in a book, watch a video, discuss the concepts with a peer, or dive into an experiment. (p. 45)

By necessity, I received a blend of in-person and radio instruction. My teacher didn't have the kind of options Novak and Tucker described. The direct instruction method, if used in isolation, might help students do well on a test but without imparting meaningful understanding of what was learned. Therefore, the optimal choice is a combination of direct instruction with other methods of blended learning, inquiry-based learning, and constructivist learning, among other methods.

Do you believe that there is a best practice pedagogical approach to meet the instructional needs of every one of your students?

Effective literacy development is one of the most important tasks of teachers, particularly those teaching students with similar challenges to what I would have faced if dropped into a US seventh grade. Researchers have found that the combination of interactive and direct instruction works well with ELL students. Do you think this approach in your class would be effective with your ELL students or any other group of students?

What pedagogical approaches resonate most with your experience as a teacher? Why? And what are the approaches that resonate the least for you? Why? Which of the pedagogical approaches you know do you think will work with a student like me in your classroom?

Imagine that you were born into a family like mine in the hamlet. How would your life be different? What would be similar to the life you are living? Assuming that you had moved to the US when you were 11 years old, what do you imagine school would have been like for you?

Reference

Novak, K., & Tucker, C. (2021). *UDL and blended learning: Thriving in flexible learning landscapes.* Impress.

65

Chapter 5

From the hamlet to Seward Park High School

"Time has been transformed, and we have changed; it has advanced and set us in motion; it has unveiled its face, inspiring us with bewilderment and exhilaration."

Khalil Gibran

I already knew from experience that time moved in different ways at different times. Time moved slowly when I was growing up in the hamlet. Then it seemed to speed up between the day in March 1975 when we took my mother to the airport and the bright Sunday afternoon in April 1977 when I flew with my brother Arsenio from Santo Domingo to John F. Kennedy Airport in New York. In the days immediately before boarding the airplane, time flew in a blur. Then came New York time!

Everything changed for me. I had stepped, as if through a doorway, from a small village deep in the Caribbean countryside to the capital of the world; from a small farm where the sun kept the time to a city with clocks attached to walls and buildings everywhere; from living in a hut to living in a big building; from a poor Caribbean island nation to the most powerful nation on Earth. I left Santo Domingo on a hot, sunny day and I arrived in my new home on a cold, rainy New York afternoon.

My first days of becoming an American were a whirlwind of emotions and new realities: pain, joy, confidence, uncertainty, acceptance, rejection, freedom, hate, and love. But that is the American story, the one I wanted to pursue.

My senses were on high alert. I desperately tried to understand the strange sounds I was hearing for the first time. The sound of people speaking English and other languages didn't bother me as much as stranger sounds coming from everywhere else: doors, fire trucks, police cars, and ambulances; and the strangest and most disconcerting of all, the sound of the subway trains passing right beneath the apartment building where we lived at 127 Ludlow Street on the Lower East Side in Manhattan.

It was as if the laws of nature had changed and I traveled back in time to the time when I was a baby. I looked at everything with great curiosity. The buildings, the traffic, the people rushing everywhere without any time to say hello—everywhere I looked I saw something that threw me off balance. Before sunrise I looked for the dawn, and in the late afternoon before sunset I looked for the dusk. I saw neither one.

On the day after I arrived, my mother and my brother Digno went to work and left me feeling painfully lonely in the apartment. Where was I? Where were my trees and the animals on the farm?

I looked out the windows and saw many people walking about. I considered going outside. My mother told me that the neighborhood was dangerous, but I was feeling trapped in the apartment so I ignored her warnings and went out.

It was my first encounter with many new odors, some pleasant and some unpleasant. As I approached the block between Broome and Grand Streets, where the school that I came to love was located, I smelled something foul that I would later learn was marijuana. Where Ludlow Street ended at Houston Street, I smelled all kinds of pleasant things coming from the famous Katz's Delicatessen. People were coming and going through the door. I walked back and forth, lifting my nose to smell everything that I could capture as if I were a puppy.

During those first days, which became weeks and then months, I understood little of what was being said around me. In stores, I was often told, sometimes in a loud voice, to "Speak English!" I understood what they wanted, but I was unable to meet the request. It didn't matter that I wanted to please them; I felt incompetent and out of place.

Fortunately, the combination of my curiosity and my desire to please kept me engaged. I carried around a little book of basic English my brother had given me. I had landed in the land of opportunity, and I desperately missed being able to communicate. I missed the familiar surroundings of my hamlet and the people I loved. But my mother's love and determination were always my inspiration in this new world, and I pushed forward and accepted what I had to leave behind.

As I began the process of adaptation into a more complex society, my yardsticks for measuring success changed. Even crossing the street was a complex high-stakes challenge. I spent much of my first days in the city with one or the other of my brothers at their workplaces, where I picked up odd jobs. The owner of an antique store in the building where Arsenio was the "super" would hire me to clean furniture he was selling. I was surprised to learn that old things could be more valuable than new ones.

Earning $20 for a day of work at the Spanish restaurant on Orchard Street where my brother Digno worked was both a luxury and a new measure of success. I was proud to be able to send money to my grandmother in the Dominican Republic. It gave me joy to do for her what Arsenio had been doing for us for so many years.

Arsenio introduced me to exciting sights and adventures beyond the Lower East Side. We took the ferry to the Statue of Liberty. He took us on Sunday drives out of the city to places like Bear Mountain, where we would relish the country air and look out on the mighty Hudson River far away from the city's crowds and noise and smells. He took me through the Lincoln Tunnel, under the same mighty river. Arsenio teased, "Now you've crossed a river without getting your feet wet. What a privileged boy you are."

During these first months, we also toured the city in Arsenio's old Impala—Central Park, the wealthy life on Fifth Avenue, the homeless who lived on the Bowery. He took me to my first professional baseball game—he clearly wanted to seal the deal and make me happy to be in New York.

I learned to ride a bicycle, which was not as gratifying as riding my Rainbow but it was an exciting adventure. It was a great day when I was able to buy my own used bike, but along with that came another new feeling—the fear of losing this new possession. My friend Christopher had been accosted by gang members who stole his bike. I learned the price of having possessions in this new land. I began to adjust to the complexities of living in this very large city.

From a young age, I had derived my self-worth from work and the contribution that I made to my family. I got my first full-time job in New York just before the start of the school year through the recommendation of a Dominican neighbor on the Lower East Side. It was as a dishwasher at Maxwell's Plum, which the New York Times later described as "a flamboyant restaurant and singles bar that, more than any place of its kind, symbolized two social revolutions of the 1960s—sex and food..." (Miller, 1988). I'd already come a very long way from my hamlet! At Maxwell's Plum I learned a number of life lessons that were not offered at Seward Park High School where I would be enrolling.

Bolgen Vargas

High School Senior Picture

Although my English was still very poor, my work ethic was appreciated and I was promoted from dishwasher to busboy. That meant getting a portion of the tips from the waitstaff, and it exposed me to more English language than I heard washing dishes. And Maxwell's Plum gave me a window to a more privileged life. It was an opportunity to learn more about a culture with which I was totally unfamiliar. I watched and listened. I was living in a state of profound culture shock.

According to one definition, "Culture is the system of shared beliefs, values, customs, behaviors, and artifacts that members of society use to cope with their world and with one another and that are transmitted from generation to generation through learning" (Bates & Plog, 1990, p. 7).

The difference between the Dominican culture I'd grown up with and the American culture I'd been dropped into was, of course, enormous. For instance, in the Dominican Republic, we feed our dogs the same food that we eat, so when I was working at the restaurant and was asked to put leftover food in a "doggy bag," I assumed it was actually for a dog—and, by the way, that American dogs ate pretty nice pieces of steak. Then I learned that Americans mostly buy specific dog food and that they also give their dogs showers and buy clothing for them. I was confused by all this and thought that our way made more sense.

I was also dismayed when I used one of the first sentences I learned to conjugate: "How are you?" "¿Cómo está usted?" I was able to use the sentence clearly in a way that was understood even with my accent. But people would respond with one-, two-, or three-syllable sentences such as "Fine," "Okay," or "I'm doing good." In the Dominican culture, particularly in my hamlet, when you ask a person, "¿Cómo tú estás?" or "¿Cómo está usted?" you can expect a long reply such as, "I feel that I am in good health but I am concerned about my mother's health" and then perhaps a long history about how the family is doing. And in the middle of telling this story, the person might reveal that he isn't sleeping well because he is thinking too much about his mother's health and wishing he had enough money to take his mother to the doctor.

So, prior to entering Seward Park High School, I was living with culture shock every day. There was not a day during which I didn't struggle to make sense of the environment of my newly adopted city. But with each week that passed, my disorientation diminished a little.

After four months sheltered by my family, in the fall of 1977, I enrolled at Seward Park High School. I had already learned how to ride a bike, I had held a job, I had learned a few English phrases ("thank you" being a most important one). And now I would have to become more independent, navigating the world without being attached to my family. On paper I was the right age for starting the ninth grade, but I believe I was, in fact, one or two years older than that.

I had never entered a building as big as my new school—just one more culture shock for me. Seward Park High School occupied an entire block, bounded by Ludlow, Grand, Broome, and Essex Streets, on the Lower East Side. I shared my high school experience with a diverse student population of more than 3,000 fellow students: African American, Latino, Asian, Eastern European—immigrants, like me, or the children of immigrants, the children of poor and working-class families. In addition to English, the student body spoke in Spanish, Mandarin, French, Russian, Hindi, Punjabi, Polish, Ukrainian, and Vietnamese, among other languages. The cultural diversity resembled the world and, of course, the city. As I discovered, my school had an extraordinary faculty of dedicated teachers, guidance counselors, and staff.

In my first days at Seward Park, I walked the halls with a broad smile, knowing about 200–300 words of English. Behind my smile, I felt great trepidation. Students turned to look at me when I passed, probably wondering why I seemed so happy to be in school. What they didn't know was that my big smile was hiding a big fear of this new, terrifying experience. I desperately wanted to succeed here, but I had no idea how. Fortunately, my first stop on my first day in Seward Park was Room 114, a few steps from the school entrance.

At 7:31 a.m., in Room 114, I met Ms. Diana Acosta, a caring and talented mathematics teacher who would also be my bilingual counselor. Ms. Acosta greeted me in Spanish with a warm and gentle smile. After a brief chat about my schooling and my family, she handed me a schedule and told me I was going to do well here.

"You just have to work hard and you will learn a bit of English sooner than you think, and then you will keep learning and never stop," she told me.

Learning to speak and write English was my greatest fear. What if I simply could not? Ms. Acosta spoke to me as if she had known me a long time. Unlike my Spanish, hers was perfect, and I suspected that her English was perfect too. She reminded me of my beloved teacher back home, Juan Ramos, the only person I knew in my hamlet who spoke perfect Spanish. He'd always had an optimistic view of his students. Ms. Acosta seemed to be as caring and optimistic as Maestro Ramos. I was lucky. They both viewed their students as youngsters with great potential, whereas others might have seen us as poor, immigrant, semiliterate, non-English speaking, disadvantaged, minority, and worst of all, intellectually incapable. These labels are dangerous.

However, optimism is as contagious as a smile. I left Ms. Acosta's office with my schedule—beginning English, physical education, homeroom, biology, lunch, history, algebra, Spanish—and a late pass to my first class. The first day in a new school is a terrifying wonder. My eyes were wide and my mouth was mostly shut.

At Seward Park High School I began to learn more about the American culture, such as that religion is a private affair, that girls could ask boys out, and that a brief passing exchange with a smile is okay.

I still worked at Maxwell's Plum from 4 p.m. to midnight, five days a week. At about 3:15 p.m., I took the bus to the restaurant at First Avenue and 64th Street. I was efficient with my time and did homework during lunch and on the bus. The hardest part of my day was returning home so late at night, because my neighborhood was dangerous—a high-crime area, with drugs, gangs, and lawless activities at night, even assaults and killings.

It wasn't easy working full time while attending school. I quit the job at the first opportunity. A Dominican coworker, a dishwasher who was much older, asked, "Why are you quitting your job? You're making good money. Why would you do that?" I told him that I wanted to put all my effort into school. He thought that didn't make a lot of sense.

What made it possible for me to give up the job was that my mother had gained access to a public housing apartment for low-income families with a much-reduced rent, fewer rats, and a great view overlooking a beautiful park and the East River. Between the little money my mother made babysitting, my father made standing watch part time for a clothing store, and I made working various odd jobs, we were able to cover our basic needs. Like the precarious experience of living on a subsistence farm, our financial insecurity reinforced my aspiration to pursue a different path through education.

The more time I spent in school, the more interesting it was to me. There was no high school in my hamlet, and now my school was practically around the corner. I was intent on making the most of it. I had always been fortunate to have so much support—from my mother, siblings, and maestro, and now the support I'd get from great teachers, administrators, and staff, I was inspired to immerse myself fully in this new existence. Maybe I was more fortunate than some of my peers who did not have as much support from so many sources.

Despite the fact that Seward Park was such a large high school, lacking the kind of resources in surrounding affluent communities, we did have teachers and administrators who had high expectations for our success and treated me and their other students with unconditional positive regard. Time was revealing itself to be my friend on the path to adjusting to my new world. And time would change me too.

For me, one of anthropologist Margaret Mead's (1963/1935) most striking ideas is this: "If we are to achieve a richer culture, rich in contrasting values, we must recognize the whole gamut of human potentialities, and so weave a less arbitrary social fabric, one in which each diverse human gift will find a fitting place" (p. 322). My search for the places where I fit began with the relentless support of teachers like Ms. Acosta, Mrs. Carbonara, and Ms. Goldberg, who encouraged me to explore a world that was not easily accessible to me as the first in my family to cross the cultural and educational boundaries of our traditional world.

It was Mrs. Carbonara who selected me to become one of the Seward Park dean's aides, which conferred on me a status I'd never experienced before. I was selected because I was a good role model. With this honor came the expectation that I would continue to attend school every day, exhibit excellent behavior, and always produce my best academic effort. One of my responsibilities was to make phone calls to the homes of Spanish-speaking families of students who had been absent from school. Dean's aides escorted students to the dean's office when she needed to see them. A great benefit of the job was that it gave me the opportunity to develop close friendships with two other dean's aides, José and Nelson, who had similar values. The yearbook picture captioned "The Dean's Aides" that I showed my mother, and then many years later, my wife, is one of me with Nelson, who became a lifelong friend.

The friends I developed through the dean's aide program had similar commitments and values, and we spent our free time going to movies and museums and exploring the city. On rare occasions I might escape the city by taking the F train from Delancey Street to Coney Island to jump into my beloved ocean and enjoy the ocean breeze. Most important to me, and to my mother, was that I would learn English, do well in school, and contribute to the family finances. The fact that I was perhaps two years older than most of my peers gave me a maturity that helped me to focus on these life priorities and end-goals.

I was fortunate that Seward Park provided instruction in English and Spanish. There are multiple models of bilingual education: my school offered the transitional bilingual education model so, for the most part, I received instruction in Spanish for content areas while learning ESL. The first content class that I was able to handle fully in English was Regents Math in 10th grade. By the time I reached 11th grade, my classes in math, typing, science, and accounting were in English. The transitional bilingual model aims to help students develop proficiency and literacy in English. I was also placed in a remedial reading class.

When I began my final year of high school, I was not thinking about attending college, believing that just finishing high school was the goal and a huge victory both for me and for my family. This was what my mother had worked so hard to make possible for me. Ms. Acosta thought otherwise. She could assess my work ethic and potential. I had the good sense to trust my teachers, particularly Ms. Acosta, so I did not close my mind to the idea. I knew she always wanted to do what was best for me.

Even when she accidently placed me in an advanced English class my senior year, it was an error that turned out to have consequences that have lasted to this day. I realized I was in the wrong class from the first minute, but I didn't say a word. It wasn't difficult to see the difference between that class and my prior English classes, beginning with the expectations the teacher, Ms. Judith Goldberg, outlined on that first day. The number of books we'd be required to read was three times as many as for my previous English classes, and class participation was mandatory.

There were no other students in the class with an accent like mine, an accent so strong that the first word out of my mouth would instantly announce that I didn't belong there. I succeeded in keeping silent for about a week.

Then, finally, Ms. Goldberg asked me to answer a question about a character in the novel we were reading. I believe it was *The Great Gatsby* by F. Scott Fitzgerald; a great book about power, greed, the American dream, and, among other things, great fiestas. Despite the fact that many of the words in the book were unknown to me, I was intrigued by the class discussion, by the thinking and the maturity of the students.

I did my best to answer Ms. Goldberg's question. However, there was a painful stillness in the room when I finished speaking. I knew that everyone believed that I didn't belong in that class. I was both right and wrong.

At the end of the class, Ms. Goldberg asked to speak with me. She went over a few questions in a dignified manner as if she were acutely aware of my deep embarrassment and disappointment. We both agreed that I was in this class by mistake. Ms. Acosta looked into changing my English class but said it would also require changing my entire schedule. At this point, Ms. Goldberg asked me if I was willing to work very hard to try to keep up with the class.

"I will help you," she said, "but if you fail, then you fail." That opportunity changed the trajectory of my life.

Ms. Goldberg gave me the chance to discover a lifelong appreciation and understanding of the impact that literature has in our lives. There were many times I got lost trying to understand the readings, the words, the context, the settings, and the plots of our readings. The most challenging of all was trying to understand American slang and idioms.

When reading *The Great Gatsby*, no amount of effort could help me unscramble idioms such as "pulling my leg" or "voice is full of money." "Heart-to-heart talk" held some meaning for me. Some of the slang phrases were even harder for me to understand: "lay off" (stop the nonsense), "razz" (make fun of), "shiv" (knife). My struggle with these words gave me insight into my own communication dilemma in the diverse Spanish-speaking world of New York. I struggled to get my point across when I used Dominican slang with non-Dominicans. Some Dominican slang was almost impossible to translate into English.

It was as if Ms. Goldberg intended to create a feast of books, poems, and rich conversation for hungry and deprived children like me. She was brilliant, knowledgeable, and devoted. Most important, she knew each of our backgrounds: some of us were breadwinners, some of us were citizens, some of us were immigrants, and some had books at home and some did not. However, above all she saw our humanity and the potential in all of us. She had a natural appreciation of the funds of knowledge each of us brought to the classroom.

We ended the year reading the novel *Ethan Frome* by Edith Wharton, a story set in the fictional small New England town of Starkfield, Massachusetts. I was intrigued by the title character, who, like my father, was a subsistence farmer and indecisive about important decisions that had life-changing consequences.

I submitted my final term paper on *Ethan Frome* to Ms. Goldberg with great misgivings. I was a very poor writer, my sentences were awkward and fragmented, and my spelling was atrocious. (But at least with spelling, I had a best friend to help me—the dictionary.) There was no question that reading was easier for me to command at a proficient level with the help of the dictionary. Sure enough, about a week after submitting my paper, Ms. Goldberg returned it completely marked up with corrections and helpful suggestions. I earned a grade of C- on the paper and a C for the course.

Overall, my high school average was 87, equivalent to a B+, but I was happy with my C- on the term paper because it was the hardest assignment in my entire four years of high school. It offered me a first look at what it would take to succeed in college. Although my performance on the paper, highlighted in red pen corrections, rattled my confidence, the confidence my counselor, teachers, and my two best friends, Jose and Nelson, had in me was unwavering. Ms. Goldberg had opened the door for me to peek into the world of higher education—a world of ideas, language, philosophy, humanities, and science—a world in which to discover one's potential.

She strongly emphasized reading outside the class assignments. I got hooked by her enthusiasm. She introduced me to Ms. Wortman, one of the school librarians, who had a warm and friendly smile. Ms. Wortman taught me how to select books to read for pleasure, and how to use the library for research and term papers. But the most important thing she did was to encourage me to get a library card from the New York City Public Library. There, I had access to as many books as any student in the world. Imagine! A kid who never owned a book before! In addition, in the summer it was one of the coolest places to be and one of the warmest in the winter. And the library was also the safest place in the city—no one went there to cause trouble. To this day, I carry my NYC Public Library card in my wallet.

Ms. Goldberg also took us beyond her books and the classroom. She understood that many of her students did not have families who visited the great museums in the city or attended the theater on Broadway. However, she knew that these experiences would open other worlds to us. She arranged field trips to the Metropolitan Museum of Art and encouraged us to go to the theater. She adopted me into her family and her world and became a lifelong friend.

Ms. Goldberg is a good example of a teacher who gets to know her students and their cultures. She visited my family and got to know them well, so she had a good understanding of my family's values, strengths, and limitations. Certainly not all teachers can do what she did, and not all students have the need for such attention, but for a student like me, with multiple adversities, it made all the difference.

The more a teacher can tap into the funds of knowledge students like me bring to school from their unique experiences, the more likely the student will achieve and reach their potential. However, as I observed in chapter 1, we must also consider the well-being and workload of teachers and staff and not simply add more expectations. Teachers who are able to tap into the diversity of experience a student brings to class are better able to respond to the instruction needs of that child. I was lucky to have a teacher like Ms. Goldberg, who gave me support that made it possible for me to succeed in high school and then in college.

Even though I was working like crazy to keep up with my advanced English assignments, I agreed after all to try for admission to college.

Because Ms. Acosta had more than 400 students in her caseload, she wouldn't have the time she'd need to help me get through the complicated and, for me, very intimidating process of identifying appropriate colleges to apply to and then preparing and making my applications. So, she connected me to Talent Search, a federal program designed to find students who might make it to college with extra help.

It was February during my senior year when I first met with my Talent Search counselor, Ms. Morales, a brilliant, completely mission-driven young woman of Puerto Rican descent. She helped me select the colleges that would be a good match for me and then helped with my admission applications and financial aid forms, none of which were simple tasks.

I discovered that Ms. Acosta had already enrolled me in an SAT preparation class. With these encouraging breezes at my back, I pushed ahead. Every student in my SAT prep class had the same goal: to achieve a score that would allow entrance to a four-year college. My greatest challenge was that I didn't have an extensive vocabulary of the words I was likely to find on the SAT. But the preparation worked. I did just well enough to keep my chance for college admission alive.

Much later, when I was a school counselor, whenever I thought back to my SAT experience I renewed my commitment to be sure that all my students knew they could pursue their full potential—as students and as human beings—regardless of any test score.

I knew when I took the SAT, from the loving words and encouragement in the gentle voice of my mother, from my teachers and other loved ones—and certainly I know now from my education and experiences—that my SAT score was not a reflection of my potential but rather of the limited early education opportunities I'd had growing up in an impoverished third-world country. Too often, the public judges schools and teachers by the test scores of their students when these scores are really a reflection of the condition and limitations of the students' life experiences.

Two days after I graduated from Seward Park High School, the key to my future arrived in the form of a letter that I stood stock-still to read over and over again. "Congratulations, you have been accepted to the State University of New York College at Brockport." My admission was through the New York State Educational Opportunity Program (EOP).

I immediately let State University of New York (SUNY) Brockport know I would attend their EOP summer program on campus, starting on June 29, which was one of the conditions for admission outlined in the package accompanying the acceptance letter.

Years later I asked the woman who had been the director of admissions at Brockport, and had since become a friend, why she admitted me and even hired me as a work-study student in her office, considering my B+ high school average but very low SAT scores.

Without hesitation and with her beautiful smile, she said, "We accepted you based on your potential." I was speechless.

Reflection and Imagine Activity

I brought multiple issues to Seward Park High School: English language barriers, lack of education and other resources at home, lack of knowledge of the American culture, and issues of adaptation to name a few. Therefore, no single instructional approach, educational program, or one teacher alone could meet my complex educational, social, and emotional needs.

Have you ever taught a student with similar characteristics to mine? If yes, what lessons have you learned that could help improve the curriculum for, instruction of, and assessment of recent immigrant populations? If not, what lessons can you draw from my experience as a recently arrived student at Seward Park High School?

Do you believe that students like me should have access to high-level courses? If yes, would you have to design such a course or are they available in your school but not offered to ELL students?

Ending up in Ms. Goldberg's class by accident was one turning point in my life. What impression do you have of Ms. Goldberg as a teacher? What impression do you have of me as a student? Would you advocate for a student like me to participate in rigorous academic courses? What are the arguments against that course of action?

Imagine that you are a high school teacher teaching an advanced English class for a select group of students, and an ELL student ends up in your class by accident. Could you give them a chance to stay in your class instead of moving them to a lower-level English class?

Imagine that you, as my teacher, had ample preparation time during the school day and freedom over the use of time for planning, curriculum work, consultation, and collaboration with colleagues, parents, and students. In what ways would this increase your capacity to support me? Have you, as a teacher or administrator, experienced these conditions and, if so, in what ways does it contribute to students' and teachers' success?

References

Bates, D. G., & Plog, F. (1990). *Cultural anthropology.* McGraw-Hill.

Mead, M. (1963/1935). *Sex and temperament in three primitive societies.* Apollo.

Miller, B. (July 11, 1988). Maxwell's Plum, a '60s symbol, closes. The New York Times. https://www.nytimes.com/1988/07/11/nyregion/maxwell-s-plum-a-60-s-symbol-closes.html?pagewanted=all

Chapter 6

How did that happen?

"The privilege of a university education is a great one; the more widely it is extended the better for any country."

Winston Churchill

On June 29, 1981, I got up at 5 a.m. It was a perfect early summer morning in New York City. I packed my belongings in the big green bag my mother used for sending clothes to the family any time one of my brothers or sisters traveled back to the Dominican Republic.

I hadn't slept much the night before. My mind was too preoccupied with my departure to SUNY Brockport, 350 miles away. My mother made my favorite breakfast of *platanos* (plantains) and *avena caliente* (hot oatmeal milk). She told me she would pray for me and that if I worked hard and behaved myself, everything was going to be all right. At about 6 a.m., Nelson and José came to walk me to the subway. I would take the F train to West Fourth Street and then transfer to the A train to go to the Port Authority Bus Terminal. My mother walked me to the elevator and with a sweet, motherly kiss said, *"Ve con Dios, mi hijo"*—Go with God, my son.

When I arrived in Brockport, a college town with a population less than 10,000, Mr. Michal Peace, a gentle, spiritual, and insightful EOP counselor and mentor, greeted me warmly. He took me and the other arriving EOP students to our dormitory. I was tired and hungry, but I tried to maintain my smile and optimistic attitude. As we walked from Main Street, where we'd gotten off the bus, to Bradley Hall, my dormitory, I saw that the village was quiet and very clean with beautiful gardens surrounding the houses. There were no tall buildings and I detected no hint of a police presence. The clean air and soft breeze felt familiar to me, like those of my hamlet.

Once again, my world completely changed in the hours between early morning when I got on the bus in Manhattan and late afternoon when I got off in a rural upstate village; between waking up in the Lower East Side of New York City, a legendary immigrant neighborhood, and waking up the next morning in Bradley Hall.

I had never traveled so far by land, and I had never seen such endless luxuriant green land. I thought the soil must be very rich, and the abundance led me to think that in America everyone could have enough land and everyone could be fed. My roommate for the summer had grown up on a farm outside of Brockport. It was inconceivable to me that an immigrant from the Dominican Republic would end up with a roommate from this abundant country, both with similar levels of educational and economic disadvantage. We got along well despite some communication challenges, mostly attributable to my heavy accent.

When I came home at the end of the summer, declaring to my mother that I was now a full-time college student, she gave me such a heartfelt smile full of pride that it carried me all the way through my four years of college.

Nonetheless, college was hard work. I spent most of my four years at SUNY Brockport in the library with my dictionary open at my elbow.

I kept working on my ability to think like a college student and to read and write like a college student. And I made strides toward those goals. The first semester was the most difficult; after that, I did much better at each of my goals. By the time I graduated, I had learned that my first draft of any writing was awful, my second draft was okay, and my third was recognizable in terms of grammar and syntax. But I knew that the quality and relevance of my ideas, contexts, and concepts were reliably competent and unambiguous.

In my Political International Economy class, the final exam was a combination of multiple-choice questions and short essays. I thought I did well on the multiple-choice questions but poorly on the essays. Professor Bretton handed back the graded exams but mine had no grade, only a note: "See me after class."

He told me that I had, in fact, done well in the multiple-choice questions and that he'd mostly understood my written answers but that the grammar was so terrible that he didn't want to give me a grade because he knew I could do better. He said that he would make an exception for me because he could see that I was still mastering English. I could come to his office by appointment and correct my errors so that he could give me a fair credit. I was grateful for a second chance but anxious about correcting my grammatical mistakes. When I appeared at the scheduled time, he handed me my blue book and told me I had an hour to rewrite the essays. Once I realized I could see the errors that were, for the most part, obvious, I felt more confident that I could correct the essays and receive credit for the content. Spelling and fragmented sentences were always my Achilles heel in written examinations. Professor Bretton had given me the benefit of the doubt.

I learned that I love the world of ideas—the world of books, debate, and argument with just words, no weapons or fists. To my surprise, my favorite class was an English class titled "Visions of Other Worlds." We read seven books, including *1984* by George Orwell, *Utopia* by Sir Thomas More, *Gulliver's Travels* by Jonathan Swift, and *The Lord of the Flies* by William Golding. For one assignment, I wrote a paper on the Utopian education system. A key element in my vision for a Utopian education was that to meet high school graduation requirements, every student must work for one year on a farm. As in More's *Utopia*, this would ensure that all members of society would have one noble thing in common—farming.

I realized that my life experience living off the land had given me a valuable perspective. I could relate to the rural surroundings of the college, to the people with rural backgrounds I met there, and to the references to farming and the countryside I encountered in literature.

I was born to work with my hands and my muscles. The world of ideas was not the place for a poor boy like me. However, first in high school and now in college, I was being encouraged to see that I could live in that world, a world I hadn't even known existed until I came to the US. I started to imagine that I might be able to make a living in the world of ideas—understanding that whatever I hoped to do had to involve a job. College showed me that I could enter the world of work using knowledge rather than muscle. However, I never lost my appreciation and understanding of the significance of working with hands and muscles. I always felt secure in that world, and I knew it could always be my back-up plan. I never doubted that all work is dignified.

Then, after four years, I was a college graduate looking for a job.

College senior photo

I saw a notice that the Puerto Rican Youth Development and Resources Center (PRYD) in the city of Rochester, New York, near Brockport, was seeking a bilingual youth counselor to provide advocacy and academic counseling to Hispanic students at Franklin High School and to serve as an advisor to the Latin American Youth Coalition. The organization's mission was "to act as an advocate for and enhance the quality of life of Hispanic children, youth and their families and to build a better community." I wanted to be a part of that. And I got the job.

One aspect of the job that particularly appealed to me was supporting school attendance to help students stay in school and graduate. I'd seen many students drop out while I attended Seward Park High School and I knew the harsh consequences most of them encountered in an increasingly complex society and economy.

My work for PRYD exposed me to one of the most vulnerable high school populations in the city of Rochester. I connected well with the kids and families I met.

Less than a year later, I was offered a position in the same agency working with yet another vulnerable population, children with disabilities.

I learned a lot. I enjoyed advocating for students, and my colleagues in the agency were completely dedicated to the mission of advocating for individual students and working to change systemic issues that were adversely impacting kids. I was gaining significant knowledge about education law and policies and getting experience defending family rights to due process in administrative hearings. I became fully aware of the complexity of the struggles faced by parents and others seeking to achieve equal treatment for all kids. I met educators and community leaders who were extremely concerned about disadvantaged students.

However, after about a year in this job I was recruited away, this time to work for the SUNY Brockport Educational Opportunity Center (EOC) as a bilingual counselor in a grant-funded pilot program, the Business Outreach Program, working to help single mothers on welfare earn GED certifications. Margaret Sanchez, who had been my supervisor at PRYD and had since moved to the EOC, encouraged me to apply for the position.

The position required a minimum of a bachelor's degree with preference for a master's degree in counseling. I made it through to a final interview. The committee was impressed with my candidacy, but they weren't comfortable recommending me for the position unless I agreed to enroll in a master's degree program in counseling. Until that moment I'd never thought about graduate education. Margaret encouraged me to commit to enrolling in a master's program and spoke to the committee on my behalf. There is no doubt in my mind that I was selected because of Margaret Sanchez.

I accepted the position with a strong sense of optimism: I would find even greater meaning in the work with single mothers, and I would be better able to do so with more education. It was a double whammy of an opportunity, and I took full advantage of it.

I worked for three years in the Business Outreach Program and I studied for my master's and I continued to be active in my immediate Rochester community. And then the funding for the program came to an end and the program closed. I didn't understand how that could possibly be so, but it was. The program did a tremendous amount of good and then it simply ceased to exist!

Just five years since graduating from college, I found myself within striking distance of completing my master's in counseling education and qualifying to be a New York State certified school guidance counselor, a professional. This made it easier for me to cope with the end of the EOC pilot program and the job that had given meaning to my life and, I believed, added meaning to the lives of my students.

Now I would pursue a school counselor position to help young people grow to be better students and better people and to find the things that bring meaning to their lives.

I expected to find a position as a bilingual counselor in the Rochester City School District (RCSD). I had established myself in the community and now I could use my training as a counselor to work with the kinds of kids I'd met as a youth counselor for PRYD. Friends, colleagues, and professors all reinforced my sense that someone like me could do a lot of good in a district like the RCSD with a large number of minority students.

I marched into the RCSD Human Resource Department to submit my application for a counselor position. I was contacted for an interview. The interview went well but they couldn't assure me that any counseling positions would be open before the start of the school year in September. Sadly, this seemed to be the pattern in a district with so many needy students.

A professional friend suggested that I consider applying to a posted opening for a school counselor in the Greece Central School District in a relatively affluent suburb adjacent to Rochester. I did some research on the Greece Central School District and I concluded that it would be an unlikely place for me to start my school counseling career. Indeed, there were very few minority staff or faculty in Greece. I knew that many people would see me as a product of the world of "have-nots," the world of Black and Brown, and assume I belonged in the RCSD. It didn't work out that way.

Yes, I am a product of the working class, an immigrant, a Latino, a campesino, a Dominican American, and a city dweller now. I am all that and at the same time so much more in my own understanding of myself that I would not be defined by such limited categories. I was growing. I wanted to be an active participant in the larger society of my new adopted country.

Ironically, when I started working at Greece Arcadia High School, many in my own community and, as I discovered, in my new school community, viewed me as a token Hispanic in a predominantly white district, more token than a qualified, certified professional. But despite my initial misgivings—and their and others' misapprehensions—it didn't take long for me to adapt, earn credibility, and feel that I belonged in this family.

My students in particular embraced me very quickly. I sensed their curiosity about a person who sounded so different from them. They asked me a lot of questions, mostly about where I came from and where I learned English. I enjoyed explaining that I started learning English in New York City and that I was still learning. I used my story to convey to my students that learning and education is a continuous process that does not begin or end within the four walls of a classroom or stop at the end of a course or at graduation or even if a student drops out.

When I started at Arcadia, I was assigned as the counselor for the class of 1995. Four years later, when the class graduated, they gave me a yearbook filled with beautiful notes full of gratitude and good sentiments: "I will never forget you and how you tried to make everyone happy." "Thank you for believing in me when no one else would, and thank you for getting me where I am." "Thank you for helping me throughout high school and getting on my case about applying for college." "You are a very caring person that has made a difference in my high school years."

The class of 1995 broke me in at Greece Arcadia High School. I continued to embrace each new group of advisees with enthusiasm for 16 more years. Although the students rotated through every four years, my colleagues largely stayed at Arcadia, as I did, and we learned from and supported each other while we worked through our students' and their families' needs, wants, happy times, and crises. I learned which teachers would be best for different students, and they knew that if I asked them to take on an additional student, it was in the student's best interest.

The irony that I spent 20 years in this unexpected place, a white, suburban environment, is not lost on me. It was a long, life-changing experience that taught me firsthand that we all have more in common than not. And I believe to this day that my presence in a school with such little diversity brought greater understanding and acceptance to many of my associates who might not have had such exposure if I hadn't been there. Twenty years in this "family" gave me lifelong friends. I served more than 1,500 student advisees and their families; I couldn't go anywhere in the county without running into a graduate or parent who greeted me with enthusiasm and thanks. It was an extremely gratifying time in my life, and even today I believe I would have been personally and professionally satisfied to finish my working years in this role. But curiosity and self-reflection, combined with opportunity, would lead me down another road less traveled.

Although I worked as a school counselor in a well-to-do suburban district, I was actively engaged in my Rochester community. There, I was committed to working toward equity for all students in the city school district, believing that education is both the great equalizer and, paradoxically, the great divide between haves and have-nots. Looking back, it was my experience working with kids at Franklin High School in Rochester and then at Greece Arcadia High School that fueled my energy, my consciousness, and my commitment to support high-quality educational opportunities for all kids.

I gained a reputation in the community for commitment and collaboration. My friends and colleagues in community work urged me to run for a seat on the school board of the RCSD. If I could win a seat, I thought, I could have an impact on the lives of our most vulnerable children. In 1993, I had also gained my citizenship; now I was completely grounded in the community and in my adopted country. Citizenship made it possible for me to take my professional work and my civic involvement to the next level.

I ran for the RCSD School Board, and although I had received the endorsement of a local newspaper, I lost. Several people attributed the loss to my not being a member of the Democratic Party, so I joined the party and worked as a committee person. When I ran for the school board again two years later, I won the highest number of votes in the Democratic primary and ultimately the highest number of votes in the general election. Even my Arcadia students and the staff celebrated my success.

At the time I was elected, the board had a reputation for engaging in the poor governance practice of micromanagement. It was known inside and outside the district that the board was too involved in day-to-day management issues; some district staff members were more responsive to the board than they were to the superintendent and administration. This created an environment where the lines of governance regarding the management of the organization were not clear, leading to poor accountability throughout the district. Worst of all, it fostered an unstable environment resulting in a revolving door in the superintendent's office. None of this served our students or families well. In the four years before I joined the board, the district had four different superintendents.

I became so concerned with the board's dysfunction that in 1998 I supported challengers running against some of my board-member colleagues who were supporting the status quo. The election changed board membership, and the new board elected me president. My political and leadership experience took a dramatic leap forward. We shook up the system and significantly reduced micromanagement by the board, which contributed to stronger relationships with the teachers and the administration.

I ended my school board role by plan on December 31, 2003. Eight years had been enough. Coincidentally, the next day I began to date Jill Conlon, my future wife. I made her a seven-course dinner and she kept coming back.

Jill and Bolgen 2019

We'd actually met briefly during my first year as a high school counselor when she was a director of admissions for SUNY Geneseo, representing the college to this green counselor. Now, years later, we connected on many levels, one of which was the new experiences we could share with each other because our lives had been so different. It was also exciting to discover what our lives had in common and how many values we shared. Jill had grown up in the small college town of Geneseo, New York, surrounded by farming country. Many of her high school classmates worked on family farms, as I had. One of my favorite people in the world is a classmate of hers who exuded the same work ethic and large-heartedness I knew in my own family. Jill had seen and believed, as I did, that all work is dignified.

Once, when my father-in-law and I were walking along Main Street in Geneseo, a college student came around the corner and called out, "Mr. Conlon!" Then she stopped, surprised, and said, "Mr. Vargas?!" She had been one of my high school students, now enrolled at SUNY Geneseo where Jill's father was her teacher and advisor. Jill loves the story because she says the student's reaction to us was a spontaneous demonstration that her father and I had the same love for and dedication to our students.

It was Jill who talked me into undertaking a mid-career doctoral program in educational leadership at the University of Pennsylvania. Leaving the school board and then starting a life with Jill was a significant time of transition for me. We had talked about doctoral programs and she believed in my ability and potential more than I did. This was a rare thing for me: I'm usually confident and positive.

I had been encouraged before to seek a doctoral degree because that would qualify me for educational leadership positions. However, I saw myself as a frontline worker. When Jill encouraged me to apply to the University of Pennsylvania, I heard the voice of my friend Sue Costa, an effective community activist who took me under her wing when I was a rookie professional. She had recently passed away after a brief battle with brain cancer. She had urged me to find a school administrator role where I could more directly impact the quality of schools for our city kids. Indeed, I had many supporters telling me that I could do more for kids as an administrator than by spending my entire career as a school counselor.

But the University of Pennsylvania? This was as big a leap as changing my mode of transportation from donkeys and horses in my hamlet to the subway in Manhattan. But, as my mother often said, dreams become real if you dream at night and work hard during the day—and in my family, that also meant taking advantage of the harvest moon to work a little longer.

I arrived at the first summer session of the doctoral program still filled with anxiety, asking myself if I could truly belong at an Ivy League institution. Sure enough, almost every other member of my cohort had attended prestigious undergraduate institutions, such as Harvard, Princeton, and Penn; I was reminded again how often I felt "other." But the week was invigorating and it confirmed my hope that this would be an experience that could add to my professional knowledge and ability. And, once again, I felt that my background could help me make a contribution in an otherwise fairly privileged environment. By the end of the week, I noticed that my peers and faculty were curious about my different world and appreciated my perspectives and contributions. I felt confident that I did, indeed, belong there.

I expected that the prestige of this wonderful institution would expose me to some of the best educational mentors as well as to national educators and connections. I know that some people questioned what a school counselor was doing in such a program. My formal education was quite humble compared to my cohort peers, but I thought my years on the Rochester school board, combined with my governance experience on various community boards and almost 17 years of direct service to students and families, would serve me well. And they did. It was clear to me that my professors appreciated my improbable path from third-world island hamlet to their classroom.

The program was not easy or simple. It was extremely rigorous and, given that English is my second language, success required extra diligence in my reading and writing assignments. As in my undergraduate and graduate programs, the library and those who worked there were my friends. When I was on campus I spent most of my time outside class in the library accessing support and ensuring I got as much work done as possible so that when I returned to my students at Arcadia, my head would be clear and my Penn work under control. When I was home, I would leave work at the end of the school day, walk our beloved dog Tesoro, and then head off to the library at the University of Rochester. I could get in about three hours of work before returning home to prepare dinner and then dive back into my assignments. Given the challenges of life as a farm boy on the island, working long hours for this program was not a hardship. In fact, it was easier than crossing a fast-flowing river barefoot—it wasn't a matter of life and death.

It has always made me uncomfortable to hear that if I could overcome so many obstacles to get where I am today, why can't we expect other "disadvantaged" students to do the same. In fact, I do believe that any student can achieve a high level of education if they are fortunate enough to have the bank of support that I encountered along my journey. I certainly didn't "pull myself up by the bootstraps." I am the product of the help and support that protected and encouraged me all along the way.

This understanding drove my dissertation topic, "Educational Success in the Face of Adversity as Measured by High School Graduation." I was keenly interested to research and document factors that impact the resilience of some students over others facing similar circumstances. The aim of my study was to examine the factors contributing to the success (as measured by attainment of a high school diploma and graduation) of members of the RCSD class of 2009, who had overcome multiple, documented risk factors identified in the literature as impairing their ability to achieve positive educational outcomes.

My study looked at whether students whose educational experience is affected by a combination of risks factors can go on to succeed if they experience multiple protective factors, such as caring relationships; expectations that are set within the family, at school, and/or elsewhere; opportunities for mentoring; involvement in extracurricular and community-based activities; and other forms of support that encourage optimism.

I worked steadily on my dissertation for three years. After finishing my defense in front of my dissertation committee, I left the room while the committee deliberated my fate. They accepted the dissertation with distinction. I found myself reflecting on my research about the power of hope, optimism, high expectation, and resiliency and wishing that every poor child could be as fortunate as I was to have had rivers of people filling my reservoir of support that made this day possible.

Graduation Day UPenn 2010

Every time I have a conversation about how I overcame adverse educational conditions, inevitably people bring up characterizations of me that include words like *determination, grit, resilience,* and *hard work.* I often feel that they give me more credit for my success than I deserve. Yes, determination, grit, resiliency, and hard work can take you far but, as in a baseball game, you can get a base hit, a double, or even a triple and more than 99 percent of the time the hitter behind you is what brings you home. In my case, success was largely due to people, policies, and opportunity made available to me—and a bit of luck, too.

Regarding the people who helped and pushed me along, the story I tell here is their story as much as mine. Of course, there were many more people who cared and helped and pushed than I can include here without telling the story of my life hour by hour. As I have said before, any of my successes are the product of a great deal of love, care, and encouragement.

Regarding policy, take for example the 1965 Immigration and Naturalization Act, championed by Presidents Kennedy and Johnson and finally passed by Congress. This Act replaced the 1924 Johnson-Reed Immigration Act that created a restrictive quota system limiting immigration visas to 2 percent of each nationality residing in the US. The 1924 Act favored Western and Northern European nations and discriminated against people from Asia, Africa, the Middle East, Latin America, and Eastern European nations. In 1965, there were fewer than 1,000 people from the Dominican Republic living in the United States, which meant only 20 Dominicans qualified for a permanent residency visa. Without that change in policy, my chance to settle here and lead the life I have would have been minimal.

Regarding opportunity, America made investments in me through the public education system that took me into both high school and then college, including the Educational Opportunity Program at SUNY Brockport, which supported me academically and financially. These investments ultimately provided me with great teachers who fostered my hard work, grit, resiliency, and determination and fed my curiosity for new and different experiences, all of which stretched my potential and encouraged me to go to unexpected places.

So, what do I take away from my life experience? That opportunity matters. It opens the mind, heart, and spirit and opens doors to new experience. We need to envision the best for every child's future. We need to believe in their ability to grow, and not just stop with test results and standards. We need to open doors for children to experience their potential through new and enriching opportunities, beyond what is in their backyard, to feed their curiosity. We need to ensure that one positive relationship becomes the gateway to many more, because it does, indeed, take a village to raise any of us. We need to care about every child as if they are our own.

And we need to advocate for support programs and services that can fill in to mitigate the adverse circumstances in the lives of many children, particularly those born into poverty. If we are earnest in our love for all children, and believe in their ability to grow, that they are not fixed, then we can educate every child to their full potential. I am successful (to the extent that I am) because I was touched by such love, which provided me with the self-possession to believe in myself and that what I did mattered. Never again should we accept that a child's life trajectory would be largely determined by the "ovarian luck" of birth into better or worse circumstances. We, as a society, have the ability to provide the match to light a child's curiosity rather than putting out the natural flame that resides in their heart and mind.

What lessons can I offer you from my experiences? High expectations and asset-based pedagogy matter. Caring relationships and classroom environments matter. Affirming students' identities, as my teachers did for me, matters. Multiple risk factors require support in multiple places as I found in my dissertation research. Effective school practices, such as building capacity to serve ELL students and all students, are essential. These guiding principles, drawn from my experiences, inspired me to move into education administration to build systems that support teachers in their essential work and to honor them as professionals.

Reflect and Imagine Activity

How unlikely was it for someone like me to find a road to an Ivy League institution? I was born in a third-world country without an elementary school or high school in my hamlet. I was born into a family where neither parent had attended a single day of school, with no books at home or in the hamlet, and where none of my brothers attended school past sixth grade. Later, in New York City, I lived in a stressful neighborhood with homelessness, drugs, gangs, crime, and prostitution.

Multiple supports in multiple places helped me to continue my education and earn a master's degree and doctorate and to become an educational leader. It is no wonder that I believe firmly that the influence of teachers, school counselors, and administrators is essential to educating every child and helping them be successful and develop productive lives.

However, my years of experience as an educator and a community leader have modified my belief in the absolute power of teachers and educators to shape the destiny of every child in the same way that they changed my life. So many outside variables exist, including poverty, school structure, working conditions, and toxic neighborhood environments, to name a few, that we must recognize that the influence of teachers and administrators is necessary and critical—*but it is insufficient to change the trajectory of kids' lives.*

What can schools do to help mitigate some of the risk factors that children like me bring to school? What outside support would be essential for schools and teachers to help each child succeed?

Within four years of my arrival in this great country, I graduated from high school and went on to graduate from college in four more years. I believe that my teachers and schools not only changed my world but had the power to change the world of every child. This thinking motivated me to become an educator. What motivated you to become a teacher? What sustains you to remain in the teaching profession? Have any of your beliefs or motivations changed since entering the profession?

It is easy to imagine that for a kid like me, potential could be overlooked. What are some ways you can imagine tapping into this potential? What multiple supports in multiple places would you imagine he needs that must come from outside of your classroom?

References

Immigration Act of 1924, Pub. L. 68-139; 43 Stat. 153 (1924).

Immigration and Naturalization Act Amendments of 1965, Pub. L. 89-236 (1965).

Chapter 7

Hope and possibility

In these final chapters, I widen my focus beyond my own experience as a student to take in what I learned as a professional working to address the challenges of ELL students and other students with characteristics similar to mine. Combining my life experience and professional experience with my doctoral research, I will describe some of the risk factors that can affect ELL student achievement in particular, as well as the achievement of any student facing adversities. In the course of research for my dissertation at University of Pennsylvania, I developed what I call a "gateway protective factors framework" to help explain how students like me who face multiple adversities are able to beat the odds. My research focused on success rather than failure.

My concern here is the ability and capacity of teachers and schools to help students facing multiple adversities, as well as the role of family and community in helping all students succeed in the classroom and outside of school.

My research revealed that as important as the teacher is, it takes multiple supports in multiple places to address the multiple adversities faced by many students. I hope to provide insight into my own unlikely path to success and to offer answers to the question people, teachers included, have asked me: *How did you make it while so many others with similar circumstances don't?* I believe those answers must apply widely because I was typical of students facing adversities.

Often, when a kid like me succeeds in school and in life, a common explanation is that they are "resilient." I hear this often when I interact with people who wonder about my personal and professional life trajectory: "Obviously, you are resilient." Really? It's that simple?

So, when I had the opportunity to make my own study of why, facing the same degree of adversity, some students succeed and some fail, I decided to use resilience as a framework for two research questions:

- How do RCSD class of 2009 graduating seniors who were exposed to similar multiple risk factors as their dropout counterparts— poverty, limited English proficiency, family instability, racism, and/or challenging neighborhood conditions—describe their path to educational success?

- In what ways, if any, do their answers describe developmental protective factors that support resilience and provide insights that might lead to improvement in graduation rates among populations of students who face multiple risk factors and other forms of adversity?

As I gathered answers to these two questions, I developed this hypothesis:

- RCSD class of 2009 students in my study who graduated with a high school diploma experienced a greater number of mitigating protective factors than those who failed to graduate. The graduates were thereby better equipped to overcome multiple levels of risk.

And, indeed, what I found is that students whose educational experience is affected by multiple risks factors can succeed if they experience multiple protective factors; that protective factors can break the barriers to success and increase the odds of graduating from high school.

I categorized those protective factors as:

- Caring relationships
- Expectations that are set within the family, at school, and/or elsewhere
- Opportunities for mentoring

- Involvement in extracurricular and community-based activities, and other forms of support that encourage optimism

I surveyed 608 students from the RCSD and interviewed a sample of students who graduated and students who dropped out. The participants in my study provided a rich look at their life experiences in multiple contexts (e.g., home, school, neighborhood) and perspectives and evidence essential to informing educational reform aimed at increasing graduation rates for students facing multiple risk factors.

Here are two representative examples from my study: one student who was able to overcome significant adversity to graduate from high school and a second student facing multiple adversities who did not graduate.

Student 1 (Graduated)

Student 1 is an 18-year-old who moved to the United States from Puerto Rico in 1999. He learned English in the United States, and he lives in the northeast section of Rochester, one of the most challenged neighborhoods in the city, with one sister; his mother; and his father, who is disabled. Although the family moved homes several times, he was able to attend the same school from seventh through 12th grade, giving some consistency to his educational experience. He was on a free- and reduced-lunch program at school.

Clearly, this student presented several risk factors: ELL student, high poverty, housing instability, family employment instability, many transitional situations, and unsafe neighborhood.

You may be surprised to learn that this student was admitted to one of the nation's most competitive engineering universities. So, what helped this student to beat the odds? Several protective factors were also present in his life to help mitigate the risks. First, his family valued education. His mom was a high school graduate with some college experience, and although his father dropped out of school, he went on to earn a GED certification. The student was enrolled in a bilingual and accelerated program. He talks about teachers, administrators, and a school counselor who had high expectations. He participated in community programs where he experienced leadership skills training and had job opportunities. He describes supportive friends who spent time together outside school. He had hope and goals. He describes influences in his life that combined to mitigate the adversity in his life.

In his own words:

Risk Factors

"I grew up moving around a lot. I moved from Puerto Rico to the US a couple of times."

"We've moved three times (in Rochester) and all three times have been in the last four years because of the economy."

"My dad got laid off...then he got in an accident so he can't work... (my mom) doesn't make a lot of money...she gets food stamps... so me and my sister got a job and now my brother got a job too, pretty much to pay the bills and help around the house and stuff. So it's been a little helpful but it's not a lot."

"When I was younger I used to stay inside because my parents were afraid something would happen to me. I played with my brother and my sister. A couple streets down you could find drug quarters, people selling drugs, all that stuff, but mostly I kept inside the house and around my street where people and neighbors were really nice, so it was okay."

Protective Factors

"(My mom) doesn't know a lot of English and it's been difficult for her. But she always wakes up in the morning and goes to work and goes through the day and never gives up...She's always working for us and doesn't do a lot for herself. She's always working for the family, so she is very influential."

"Teachers were always helpful...since I didn't know a lot of English they would always try to help me...I was in the Language Academy Program, which was geared toward bilingual students. Everyone was Spanish. It wasn't difficult; it was easy. But I've always had it easy doing stuff in school."

"A lot of teachers had very high expectations because we were in an accelerated program...the principal and administrators knew since we were in the honors classes they expected a lot more of us, to behave better, participate more in school activities, you know, to do better in class to be role models for the other students, I guess."

"My peers were helpful...they have always been supportive and I have always been supportive of them...we like to hang out outside of school and in school, like most teenagers do."

"I was involved in the Hillside Work Scholarship Program...they helped me get a job at Wegman's...because I've been connected at Hillside, a lot more opportunities at Wegman's have been opened to me. I've also had the Hispanic Leadership Program with the Red Cross, which basically teaches us about leadership skills... how people can make good decisions...treat other people well with respect...."

Student 2 (Dropped out)

Student 2 is a 19-year-old biracial male with an extended family in the area but a difficult home situation. With the loss of his supportive grandparents, who were always "in my corner," and then the presence of his mother's abusive boyfriend, the student was placed in a supportive foster care setting. He speaks very highly of his foster family and of being more engaged in sports and school at that time. He describes his teachers as supportive and encouraging. However, he chose to return to his home situation and describes anger issues leading to more troubling behavior.

In his own words:

Risk Factors

"When my grandfather passed, things got rough and hectic. I lived in an abusive house. My mom's boyfriend at the time was abusive. My mom wasn't very supportive."

"(At) a young age I was a troubled child...I had anger issues and a lot of self-control issues."

"(After foster care) I went home...I had trouble keeping my temper under control and just focusing...I felt like I was ready to go home, but my judgment was wrong."

"When I went home, the more trouble I got into the more I thought about my life and how it would have been if I had stayed in foster care and with my foster parents."

"I started doing things I usually didn't do. You know, grades started droppin', I started quittin' sports, skippin' classes. Just doing things I didn't do."

"All the wrong things are just piling on you. And no matter how much you have joy and love for something, with so much bad stuff on top of you, you just can't push yourself."

Protective Factors

"Growing up was, at first, it was good—when my grandfather was alive. The people that were in my corner when I was young was my aunt and my grandfather and grandmother. Before my grandfather passed and before my grandmother lost her memory, they were always in my corner."

"I have other family members (who) encourage me to do my best—great cousins. You know, they pushed me and said that education is the key to success...anything they ever told me was positive. And that warmth comforted me and made me stay solid."

"If I were to have stayed at (my third foster home), I would have finished high school, hands down. (They) encouraged me and wanted me to do my best. My foster parents, they were good people, you know? They made sure I ate well, I slept well, everything. I was healthy...They came to games and supported me."

"When I was in foster care, sports was my life. Pretty much every weekend we went from state to state within the East Coast area, and I loved it...those privileges (were why) I was doing good in school. I was passing every class always."

"I loved school. I still to this day love school."

"(Teachers) would encourage me to stay in school, make up my work, do my work. They gave me their numbers to call (if I) had any problems...."

106

"(If) something was bothering me (a teacher would) pull me aside and try to talk...there were resources there to help with my issues."

"In life (to) be married and successful...you have to have an education, you have to have a job, and then you have to meet a person that has faith."

One might wonder why Student 2 didn't succeed, given both risk and protective factors present in his life. In my study, I adopted the term "gateway protective factors" (see the figure below), to describe protective factors that operate in concert with one another. One factor may lead to another and another. By providing kids with exposure and progressive, dynamic access to other forms of protection, gateway protective factors enable them to overcome barriers presented by poverty, low expectations, family instability, and other forms of adversity. As important as any one protective factor might be—such as a caring and supportive teacher—I found that students succeed when protective factors operate synergistically in their lives. As important as any one protective factor might be, it is when this one leads to or provides access to additional protective factors that a student's chances for overcoming adversity are greatest.

Original conceptual framework modified to highlight the influence of gateway protective factors

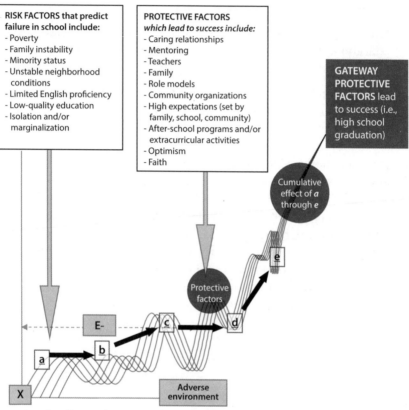

A student (X) can only escape adversity (identified here as risk factors that influence their life) and succeed if they acquire enough potential energy (E-) from protective factors to be able to do so.

Gateway protective factors identified as a through e along the trajectory:

a = *Caring relationships* with adults at school, at home, or in the community; with peers

b = *High expectations* held by adults at school, at home, or in the community; held by peers

c = *Meaningful participation* in school, at home, or within the community

d = *External assets:* positive experiences in school, at home, or within the community; with peers

e = *Internal protective factors:* Students' internal assets, such as goals, self-direction, and empathy

Risk factors were proven to push students down into adversity, and multiple protective factors were proven to help them bounce back, gain momentum, and take steps toward success.

The results of the study demonstrate the need for schools and communities to mitigate multiple adverse conditions by establishing programs and services that can provide multiple supports in multiple places. Incorporating initiatives to address such students' plights, within the broader context of educational reform, should be just as important as incorporating plans for high standards, assessment, and instruction.

Role and mindset of teachers in promoting ELL student success

Given the "village"—schools, families, communities—necessary for providing protective factors, what would be your role as a teacher or administrator in helping ELL students and other students to achieve success?

Let's face it, teachers are expected to perform in multiple roles. We expect teachers to be experts in subject matter, to deliver effective instruction, to be familiar with various pedagogical approaches, to be classroom managers, to perform student assessments and then be student data analysts, to respond to the social and emotional needs of each of their students, to be collaborative, and to inspire students to develop a love of learning. The list goes on. It is no wonder that teachers are often considered superheroes. Realistically, however, no one can meet all the expectations we impose on teachers.

So, rather than discussing all the roles teachers are expected to perform daily, I will focus primarily on what I consider the most important role for teachers of ELL students in particular, and all other students as well: establishing strong relationships with each student. The teacher mindset is a critical aspect of delivering on this role.

In my personal experience, as a student and in my professional experience as a school counselor and superintendent, I learned that one of the most effective things teachers can do is to establish caring relationships with their students. You might have heard the expression that "students don't care what you know about the subject you are teaching until they know that you care about them as a person." This is particularly true of our most vulnerable students. It sounds like common sense, and it is. However, establishing a caring relationship with each of your students is not easy. The greatest challenge is the matter of time. As Sonia Nieto observes, "Students evaluated their teachers' level of caring by the amount of time they dedicated to their students, their patience, how well they prepared their classes, and how they made classes interesting" (Nieto & Bode, 2018, p. 267).

Although a teacher may have control over being patient, being well prepared for class, and making the class interesting, they often do not have control over securing the amount of time necessary to establish a positive, caring relationship with each of their students. For example, a teacher may have multiple students in the class who need extra individual support, which may require time both during and after school. Competing for the time they might be giving, especially to vulnerable students, teachers must perform a multitude of administrative tasks outside of instruction time to respond to demands from the district central office, state and federal education departments, and school bureaucracies. Also, beyond instruction time, teachers must administer and grade excessive testing. And, of course, teachers are dealing each day with the full range of academic, social, and emotional needs of their students. Sadly, these challenges are often faced in school environments lacking resources or support from administration, the community, and the society at large.

Despite the challenges teachers face, particularly teachers working in urban environments with children facing multiple adversities, many teachers manage to establish strong relationships with their students. There is a body of research that shows that many teachers stay in toxic and broken systems *because* of the close caring relationships they have with their students and their belief in each student's potential. As superintendent of two challenged urban districts, I personally saw this kind of growth mindset—which sees all students as capable of improvement through effort (see Carol S. Dweck's [2007] *Mindset: The New Psychology of Success*)—in many of the most effective teachers. Even though they might be dissatisfied with the lack of support they felt from the school bureaucracy, the families, and/or the community, they continued teaching because they cared and were concerned for their students' academic success and well-being.

Take, for example, my own situation as a college student when my professor allowed me to rewrite my exam essay questions because he could see the quality of my content and understood that I was still developing my written English. He demonstrated a growth mindset with the expectation that, given time and opportunity, I had the potential to perform at a higher level. And I did. Not only did it make a difference to me on that one exam, it gave me confidence and experience in my ability to edit and rewrite my own work and to continue to improve.

As I reflect on all the teachers I connected with as a student and consider which ones I learned the most from, it was the teachers who had a growth mindset rather than the fixed mindset that sees students as fixed in their abilities. Teachers who believe that ability is fixed are likely to believe that a single test can measure a student's potential.

Role of the family

The role of the family has a powerful impact on any child's education, and this is not different for immigrant families. Yet it is not the same, either. The role of immigrant students' families is often misunderstood. According to research, my family was like most immigrant families when it comes to beliefs about roles and responsibilities for the education of their children. Carola Suárez-Orozco, Associate Professor of Applied Psychology and Teaching and Learning at New York University, along with two other researchers published longitudinal research about immigrant student adaptation. Their study includes views of immigrant parents and their children's teachers. They heard this from teachers of immigrant children from mainland China, Hong Kong, El Salvador, Guatemala, Nicaragua, Honduras, Dominican Republic, Haiti, and Mexico.

> We asked teachers, "How do you expect parents to support their children's education?" Many of the responses were telling. One summed up the paradigm of parental involvement: "In American schools, parents are expected to come to school and question the school. They are asked to be more active in the education process." Another teacher said she wanted " for parents, by their words and their deeds, to impress upon children that the education process is important." Coming to school was a critical

symbol of parental involvement: " I expect parents to find ways to come in to the school . . . The tendency and assumption are that they should be more invested in their children's academic work. I want my bilingual student's parents to invest more so that their children can be better students." Supporting the students' efforts at completing homework was another theme: "When I send work home, please make sure the student does it." Another said, "I expect them to help their children with their homework" (Suárez-Orozco et al., 2010, p. 76)

As I read these comments from teachers, all kinds of scenarios come to mind. Most of the teachers' expressed desires, at first glance, sound reasonable. After all, when parents are actively involved, students perform much better academically, have better school attendance, and have a better attitude toward school.

The challenge with these teachers' perceptions of immigrant parental involvement is that these parents come from different cultural, social, and economic backgrounds. Most view their role quite differently. It would have been inconceivable for my mother to question my teachers because for her teachers are always to be highly regarded and respected. She trusted that the teacher always knew best how to educate her children, and schools as institutions were to be treasured. Many immigrant families share her view. I grew up hearing from my mother that teachers were my second parents, so if I disrespect them there would be a heavy price to pay at home. Her role, as she saw it, was to send me to school every day, make sure I was well behaved, and did what I was told to do. It would not have occurred to her to be more actively involved with my schooling than that. As it happened, I didn't miss a single day of school at Seward Park High School, and one of her great joys was my perfect attendance award.

As for homework, many immigrant parents and others living in poverty are not able to help for a variety of reasons. In the case of my family, the lack of formal education, our multiple jobs, and my family's weak English language skills left them unable to support me in completing my assignments. However, that does not mean that parents like mine do not have high expectations for the educational success of their children and place a high value on that success.

To the contrary, my mother saw education as the gateway through which her children would escape poverty. This is true of many immigrant and working-class parents. My family, like most immigrant families, came to this country with the hope that their children would achieve academic and economic success. My mother and my siblings always told me how proud they were that I stayed in school and worked hard in my classes. Some of my siblings have said they wished they could have come to the US when they were school age to take advantage of the education available here. Even though my family could not give me academic support, their emotional support along with the support of my teachers went a long way to help me achieve success in school.

Reading Suárez-Orozco's work, I am struck by how, even years after I had graduated from high school, I can still recognize the voices of the students in her study. According to the study, although many of the teachers interviewed thought immigrant parents had low expectations for their children, in actuality the majority of the students had internalized their parents' high expectation for their academic success. How could that be?

It may be that many teachers are unaware of the economic and cultural situations immigrant families may be facing. Immigrant students are often rising to very high expectations including that they help support the family's basic needs, not to mention sending money back to home countries to support other family members as I did. Not all of my teachers were aware of that, and they would likely have been surprised to learn I was doing my homework on the bus on my way to work. (My own experience makes me think of all the homeless students who don't have the luxury of a quiet, safe place to complete their homework.)

The role of the family absolutely impacts the student's academic success, so it is important for schools and teachers to have an understanding of and appreciation for families' various different perceptions, particularly those of families from different cultures, and what they mean for the student in the classroom.

Role of the community and society

Learning and education do not take place only in school. This, too, sounds like common sense, and it is. Some of our first learning experiences begin in the home and in the community. However, far too many immigrant families and families living in poverty reside in communities that have limited resources and challenging conditions.

Interestingly, I never thought I was poor in America, even though my neighborhood was impoverished and my school was underresourced and overcrowded. It was not until I worked as a youth counselor for Latino kids in Rochester that I began to understand that the neighborhoods where my students lived offered fewer opportunities than those in more affluent communities and that this contributed to the barriers between them and their potential success. Many immigrant families do not have the financial means to choose where to live based on the ZIP codes that would provide the best schools for their children. According to a National Research Council and Institute of Medicine study (2000), parents believe in the impact of community (via neighborhood conditions) on their children's experiences, subsequent levels of opportunity and, ultimately, the choices they make in life. Parents with the necessary resources to strategically approach the selection of a community in which to raise their children are said to do so in an effort to influence their physical and emotional safety, achievement levels, and opportunities for friendship. Parents who lack those resources, then, are at a recognizable disadvantage when it comes to providing highly supportive environments in which their children can grow.

Despite the challenges experienced by immigrants, ELL students and all children living in difficult neighborhood conditions, teachers are often able to accomplish enormous success with many of their students. Poverty and adverse neighborhood conditions are not an absolute bar to success. However, poverty is a proven risk factor and contributor to adversity, one that leads to underachievement and high dropout rates among student populations. So how do we capitalize on what a community can provide to mitigate poor neighborhood conditions?

It is far more productive to reflect on what is possible than to blame these poor conditions. Every community I know in America has a significant number of resources that can assist students with their education. Take, for example, the public library system, which has enormous resources in the form of books and other education materials, not to mention librarian expertise, available free to students and families. If the community where you teach is like Rochester, New York, and Manchester, New Hampshire, where I served, then you have heard conversations about children who don't have books at home and lack a reading culture there. In fact, the schools and the community have resources for easily mitigating this by making enough books available to ensure that every child can take home at least one new book a month.

I brought this message to Rochester, where 90 percent of the students are on free- and reduced lunch and some 20 percent are ELLs and bilingual students. We implemented a program we called ROCRead, and we engaged community partners to promote the fundamentals of reading and provided books for elementary children to take home over the summer and to own. A program celebration brought families and their children to the Triple-A Rochester Red Wings baseball park to get a book, watch a game, and eat a hot dog. I will always remember the grateful father who thanked me, saying that he could never have afforded to bring his entire family to see a game. Every child deserves to experience a live baseball game, with a hot dog at the park, and to own their own book. My favorite memory of the day was seeing a young student in the bleachers engrossed in reading his new book.

Community-based agencies and organizations can provide support in many ways to help children mitigate adversity and develop the resilience that can help them experience academic success. Adults in the community can help students become engaged in a variety of activities such as sports, volunteering, library-sponsored events, and arts-related and work programs. These activities can enhance students' sense of meaning and purpose and allow them to make contributions to their communities as active participants. When students are engaged in meaningful activities in their communities, it lessens the likelihood of alienation and steers them away from the high-risk activities they may see in their neighborhoods. The most important thing that communities, organizations, and residents can do for youth is to provide a safe neighborhood environment for them to live in. This is, in fact, a community responsibility, which is outside the control of the teachers and schools.

Most issues facing ELL students, such as poverty, racism, challenging neighborhood conditions, and discrimination, are institutional barriers, which means they can't be corrected by individual action. However, every individual teacher and administrator is able to love and care for students and to embody hope for their success. But you won't find these words in a job description, evaluation, education reform plan or in the latest policy coming down from federal, state, and local school district directives.

As a teacher or administrator, you probably have heard people say, "I couldn't do your job." I heard that many times and often took it as a compliment, an acknowledgment of how difficult the job was. Some might ask, "How do you do your job?" To which I would reply, "I do it with love, hope, and care." My approach is influenced by Gabriela Mistral, a teacher and writer, who was the first Latin American to win the Nobel Prize in Literature. In her poem *The Teacher's Prayer* (2004), she wrote:

> Lighten my hand in punishment, and let my caresses be ever more gentle. May I reprimand in sorrow, so that I know I have given correction lovingly!

It was a guiding sentiment because on any given day, far too many of my students arrived at school with at least three hardships creating barriers to success, such as poverty, limited English language, challenging family and/or neighborhood, and disabilities.

Maintaining a growth mindset rather than a fixed mindset is a key condition for teachers and administrators seeking to help students persist against the barriers they may be dealing with each day at home, at school, and in the community. According to Gabriella Oliveira, Associate Professor at the Harvard Graduate School of Education:

> When an immigrant child without many English-language skills arrives in an English-speaking classroom, research shows that the most important factors are the teacher's mind-set, access to adults who speak the child's language and the overall environment of the school. Some educators perceive immigrant families negatively because of cultural and language differences: They focus on what the immigrant children don't know and don't have rather than what they know and what they bring to the classroom. A deficit-oriented view can lower educators' expectations of immigrant

children, which in turn can make it harder for those children to succeed academically. (2022, SR9)

Consider my experience when I entered Seward Park High School. I had not read a book other than a few textbooks in my school back in the Dominican Republic. My prior experience didn't stop Ms. Wortman, the school librarian, from introducing me to reading outside my school assignments. And some of the books I read at her suggestion sparked my dream to cross the boundaries of my daily experience and enter the larger world of written knowledge.

Seward Park High School also provided me access to loving caring adults who had an appreciation for and understanding of my native language and culture. They encouraged me to dream beyond what my family or I could have seen as possible. Ms. Acosta, my counselor, knew my vulnerabilities and my background and still had a fierce belief in my potential. So she encouraged me to aspire to go to college even though it was far beyond my dreams and even further away from my reality. She tapped into my potential, knowing that an immigrant child like me comes to this country hungry for knowledge and opportunity, and she pushed me to explore the American Dream beyond the barriers and boundaries I may have faced without even realizing they were there.

When a teacher deals with a student like me, of course their first concern is to teach basic skills in English literacy, which is appropriate as long as this does not preclude challenging the student with higher-level literacy. But far too often, students with backgrounds like mine are placed in remedial courses across all disciplines, which, unfortunately, can lead to the self-fulfilling prophecies arising from low expectations. Teachers have extraordinary power to influence the educational outcomes of students by how they view their students, and schools have extraordinary power to promote success through the opportunities they make available to all students.

Since the publication of Rosenthal and Jacobson's landmark study of the concept of self-fulfilling prophecy in 1968, a wealth of research has documented both the immediate and the long-term impacts that teachers' expectations have on students and their levels of academic achievement.

I often wonder what would have happened if Ms. Acosta and my other teachers saw me as a low-ability student rather than a student with potential to be developed. Likely I would not have been allowed to stay in Ms. Goldberg's advanced English class based on school policy and practice, which would say that I didn't belong. And I wonder where I would have ended up, because this was a turning point in my education, setting me on my path to college.

Unfortunately, in my years of experience in multiple school districts it is not unusual for policies and practices to limit opportunities for the most vulnerable children. Schools are difficult cultures to change—especially in the area of tracking practices. But if an immigrant kid like me can adapt, learn, and appreciate a new culture, shouldn't we expect schools to live up to the same?

Here is the expression of a growth mindset for her students by a first-year teacher:

> My students believe they are in classes for stupid people. They say things such as, "We can't do this. We're only '103' (low-ability class) students." Most of them ask if they can move up, and some even say they are in the retarded classes. It is important for me to not treat these students as if they cannot handle difficult work. The novel *Always Running* is not that easy of a read for ninth-grade students. Many complex topics are dealt with, and most of the teachers at my high school would tell me it is too difficult for these kids. Yet I pushed them along and helped them get by certain spots. I try to treat these students the same as I do my "college-prep" kids…Many people feel that these kids are already lost so we should not waste any time or resources on them. It is for this reason that I have asked to continue teaching the "103" students. They need someone who has not given up on them. (Oaks & Lipton, 2003, pp. 330–331)

One of the unintended consequences of a remedial or low-level class is that students may internalize the self-fulfilling prophecy of being "low level" and adopt an academic identity of low expectation for themselves. The mitigating approach is to ensure that there is a plan for students to accelerate and move on to the next level, which reflects the long-term belief in the student's potential. It is crucial for teachers and other educators to help all students, but particularly ELL, special education, and other vulnerable students, develop a strong academic identity.

In my situation at home and in my neighborhood, there was very little opportunity to acquire the academic identity of someone capable of crossing to the other side of the tracks to go to college. In my neighborhood, the school was the only lighthouse that provided me with the opportunity to acquire such an identity. I am very aware that my teachers, counselors, and administrators had to work against the realities of crime, drugs, and other social ills I saw in the streets that I walked every day in order to give me a fighting chance. My teachers' affirmation of my academic potential pulled me away from the temptations of street life.

I understand when a teacher tells me that they are overwhelmed and exhausted by the demands to meet the academic, social, and emotional needs of their students. Yes, teaching is a challenging job. But it is a job with tremendous power to add meaning to students' lives.

Reflect and Imagine Activity

As an educator, what are your thoughts about the growth mindset, the fixed mindset, and self-fulfilling prophecy?

Take a close look at the risk and protective factor framework and think about your students who are facing the multiple risk factors presented in this framework. How many of the risk factors are being mitigated by protective factors in the family, at school, and in the community?

If you have experience working with immigrant students or any other students facing multiple risk factors, how many of those students were successful at school, as measured by graduation or, if they were elementary grades, by their level of literacy and their social-emotional well-being?

What can you, as a teacher, do to communicate to students that you care? What can the school do? Do you feel that the school, community, and parents care about your own well-being and the well-being of your students? If so, what are the messages that reinforce that for you?

In this chapter I say that my teachers provided me with a strong academic identity that was not accessible to me at home. Imagine any student you encountered who was facing multiple risk factors whom you and your colleagues helped to find the gateway to a path to academic success. Does that help you get through the tough days and prevent you from experiencing the burnout that happens to some of our colleagues?

References

Dweck, C. S. (2007). *Mindset: The new psychology of success*. Ballantine.

Mistral, G. (2004). *Selected prose and prose-poems: Gabriela Mistral* (S. Tapscott, Ed. & Trans.). University of Texas Press.

Nieto, S., & Body, P. (2018). *Affirming diversity: The sociopolitical context of multicultural education* (7th ed.). Pearson.

Oaks, J., & Lipton, M. (2003). *Teaching to change the world* (2nd ed.). McGraw-Hill.

Oliveira, G. (2022, September 1). School is for hope. *The New York Times*, SR9. https://www.nytimes.com/2022/09/01/opinion/us-school-immigrant-children. html

Suárez-Orozco, C., Suárez-Orozco, M., & Todorova, T. (2010). *Learning a new land: Immigrant students in American society*. Harvard University Press.

Vargas, B. (2010). *Educational success in the face of adversity as measured by high school graduation* (Publication No. 3410470) [Doctoral dissertation, University of Pennsylvania]. ProQuest Dissertations Publishing.

Chapter 8

The place of common sense in education reform

"If something isn't blatantly impossible, then there must be a way of doing it."

Sir Nicholas Winton, British humanitarian who brought approximately 669 children from Czechoslovakia to safety in Great Britain before the outbreak of World War II.

The following passage from education historian, policy maker, and writer Diane Ravitch expresses my belief about education reform better than I can. It could be my credo.

> Genuine school reform must be built on hope, not fear; on encouragement, not threats; on inspiration, not compulsion; on trust, not carrots and sticks; on belief in the dignity of the human person, not a slavish devotion to data; on support and mutual respect, not a regime of punishment and blame. To be lasting, school reform must rely on collaboration and teamwork among students, parents, teachers, principals, administrators, and local communities. (Ravitch, 2014, p. 325)

Over the past three decades, I have experienced firsthand—as a school board member, school counselor, and superintendent of schools—a constant stream of school reform policies coming fast from 30,000 feet

121

and usually ignoring most or all of the dichotomies Diane Ravitch lists as well as her insistence on collaboration. The architects of such reform movements sweeping down on education certainly had the intention of helping children succeed, but the excessive testing and top-down accountability measures that were always hallmarks of their efforts excluded meaningful input by those most impacted—students, families, teachers, school administrators, and local communities.

As superintendent of urban school systems, one the most challenging tasks for me was to navigate the tension between federal, state, and school board policies on one side and the well-being of students, teachers, and staff on the other. Too many of the education policies of recent decades have lacked common sense. They have demonstrated very little understanding of the complexities of school systems across the nation. New York State's accountability needs, for example, are different from those in New Hampshire. The complexities and context for educating students in suburban America are totally different than those for educating students in urban America. Simply put, it does not make sense to apply the same policies, strategies, structure, and theory of action across all districts to achieve significant school improvement for student success. But this is what we have been doing for the past two decades. Sadly, we haven't seen much improvement, particularly for students living in poverty and for ELL students.

From my own experience, I do not think we are facing a hopeless situation. But we do not have to keep working on the same story until we finally get it right. There is a more effective way to think about education change. It starts at ground level with students, families, teachers, school administrators, and local communities and builds up. I have seen this approach work on a small scale and that, I would argue, is the scale where we operate most effectively. The world of students and teachers in classrooms and the schools that house them is lived on a scale where education change can be ours to manage to best suit our students' and teachers' needs.

In 2002, Congress passed the No Child Left Behind (NCLB) Act of 2001 with strong bipartisan support. This was the beginning of large-scale federal education policy reform. I was president of the Rochester

City School Board at the time and a member of the board of directors of the Council of Great City Schools, a national coalition of urban school districts dedicated to the improvement of education for children in America's inner cities. The coalition received updates on the NCLB from officials of the federal Department of Education, including the Secretary of Education, and from members of Congress while it was being drafted.

I fully supported the concept of closing the achievement gap, but I was skeptical about what I was hearing, having already experienced the poor track record of the federal government in funding its education policies. For example, we were already dealing with unfunded mandates to provide supports to students with special needs and ELL students. But I agreed with the intention to "leave no child behind," because children with special needs, children living in poverty, ELLs, and students of color had historically been overlooked and underfunded.

The NCLB asserted that too many children were not achieving to their potential, and that the test performance gap and the difference in graduation rates that existed between minority and majority student populations needed to be addressed. This was true, but the act's response emphasized results from a regime of excessive standardized testing and created an accountability system without considering the multiple factors impacting test results. For example, the NCLB mandated that all states evaluate students' performance—including ELLs who had attended school for one academic year—in English reading/language arts, and that by the 2013–14 school year all students should achieve proficiency in the state assessments.

Teachers often asked me if I believed that a non-native English-speaking student could become proficient in English in just one year. Most researchers, as well as in my own experience, would tell you this is not a reasonable expectation for most of these students, and, therefore, lacks common sense.

Similar challenges were present for students with disabilities. For example, if a student with a disability and an individualized education program (IEP) needed to use a different assessment test, such as an instruction-level test, the US Department of Education required the results to be counted as "non-proficient." Imagine how discouraging such requirements are for students, teachers, and principals in a school that may have large populations of ELLs and students with disabilities. The school does not show sufficient progress based on a standardized assessment and is labeled a "failing school." In Rochester, ELL and special education students made up more than 25 percent of our population. In some schools, these were majority populations.

An essential goal of NCLB was that all schools in the nation would provide all students "highly qualified teachers" by 2006, specifically fully certified teachers with competence in their subject areas. The lack of qualified teachers is a serious problem, particularly for the most vulnerable students. This is not a new problem. In the 1960s and 1970s, scholars, educators, and policy makers began to show that children living in poverty, children with disabilities, Black and Hispanic students, and ELL students were more likely than middle- and upper-income White students to be taught by uncertified teachers. According to Linda Darling-Hammond (2010), "Changes in the teacher qualifications available to students strongly influence student achievement, suggesting that policies that tackle the twin problems of inadequate and unequally distributed teacher quality may help improve school outcomes" (p. 44). Unfortunately, this goal of the NCLB was not achieved, and today we are in a worse situation than ever with regard to attracting and retaining qualified teachers for the most vulnerable students, particularly those living in challenging neighborhoods.

Why did we fail and why are we still struggling to solve the problem? First, this is a problem that cannot be solved without serious financial investment accompanied by multiple strategies. Darling-Hammond said that unlike the unmet promise in NCLB, when the country experienced a physician shortage in the early 1960s, Congress passed the Health Professions Educational Assistance Act of 1963 to directly address the shortage. Similar initiatives in education were effective in the 1960s and 1970s but were eliminated in the 1980s. She wrote:

> We need a federal teacher policy that will (1) *recruit new teachers* who are prepared to teach in high-need fields and locations, through scholarships and forgivable loans that allow them to receive high-quality teacher education; (2) *strengthen teachers'*

preparation through incentive grants to schools of education to create professional development schools, like teaching hospitals, to train prospective teachers in urban areas and to expand and improve programs to prepare special education teachers, teachers of English language learners, and other areas where our needs exceed our current capacity; and (3) *improve teacher retention and effectiveness* by ensuring they have mentoring support during the beginning stage when 30 percent of them drop out of teaching." (Darling-Hammond, 2004, pp. 29–30)

Instead of responding to such suggestions in collaboration with state and local districts, the federal government during both Democratic and Republican administrations continued on the path of emphasizing standardized testing to hold schools and teachers accountable, which did nothing to address the teacher shortage but made matters worse. NCLB was enacted during the George W. Bush administration, and the Obama administration continued NCLB policies while adding an education policy initiative called Race to the Top, which committed significant resources tied to designing and implementing a teacher evaluation system.

In 2012–13, as superintendent of Rochester City Schools, I spent a great deal of time, along with my staff and the teachers union, negotiating a new teacher evaluation system as required by both Race to the Top and the New York State Education Department. Five billion dollars allocated for the Race to the Top initiative was at stake. To qualify for the funds, districts had to agree to adopt the state's Common Core standards, to expand their number of charter schools, to adopt a turnaround effort for their lowest-performing schools by taking such forceful measures as removing all staff and closing the schools, and to evaluate teachers in large part by their students' test results.

Several of my fellow superintendents in neighboring districts believed there was no way to achieve an agreement with their teachers unions, particularly regarding a system to evaluate teachers largely based on student test results. In New York State, suburban and rural districts rely on their communities to fund their budgets, so they were relatively more insulated from state or federal threats to withhold or cut funding. But urban districts, such as mine in Rochester, depend on federal and New

York State funds for more than 80 percent of our budgets. Thus, I had to address the issue. I had to implement the law or lose much-needed revenue from the federal government and from New York State.

Even though I could agree that the education system needed significant change and reform, I did not believe this approach to reform would address the most important goal on our own local education reform agenda: *to create for our most vulnerable children all the opportunities that were available in middle-class communities throughout America.* Although I had to accommodate it, I was determined not to let this poorly conceived top-down reform effort distract us from our agenda.

My theory of action was that we could close the opportunity gap by providing urban students with middle-class–like schools that would include art, music, sports, extracurricular activities, and advanced placement courses. These schools would offer expanded time, year-round, for quality extracurricular and academic activities and provide good working conditions for teaching and learning, supported by a well-functioning operations system. All of this would require significant resources. Therefore, it was important to the district budget to secure the promised funding from Race to the Top.

To the surprise of many, I was able to reach an agreement with the Rochester Teachers Association (RTA). Adam Urbanski, president of the RTA, had doubted we could agree on a way forward. He outlined several concerns on behalf of teachers and students. That multiple factors outside the control of teachers could impact test results was a strong argument against evaluating teachers by those test results. He also raised the obvious lack of consideration in the law for how to evaluate teachers of art, music, and physical education. Also, and critically, he was concerned about how such evaluation by test results could be fair to teachers who work with our most vulnerable students—ELLs, special education students, homeless students, students with chronic attendance issues—who were, in fact, a large percentage of students in our schools. Although the national- and state-level reform agendas had good intentions, they could not realistically be applied to our urban student population without accommodation for special circumstances. This is evidence of what I now call "the death of common sense in education reform."

I concurred with Urbanski's concerns and implored him to work with me on solutions. My assertion was that if we could mitigate the problems within the parameters of the law, then we could reach an agreement. I told him, and through him the teachers he represented, "I will not fight with you. If it is legal, we can reach an agreement." We had a trusting relationship, and we reached an agreement in detail. We were the first school district in New York State to submit a new teacher evaluation system to the state Education Department. It was accepted with minor changes. Most important for our students and teachers, we secured the resources to proceed with investing in our own reform agenda.

As much as we had to comply for the benefit of our vulnerable urban district, in reality I understood that the law we were complying with was not likely to survive long. Indeed, there was subsequent bipartisan agreement in Congress as part of the Every Student Succeeds Act (ESSA) of 2015 prohibiting the type of teacher evaluation we had worked hard to agree to. The law put a stop to teacher evaluation by student test scores, but it continued to put a disproportionate amount of weight on standardized tests to measure student achievement and grade our schools.

I am not against standardized testing. What I am *for* is testing standards that, when appropriately used, will foster a high-quality education and will focus us on providing the necessary conditions, support, and flexibility for teachers and students to succeed. This goal would redirect the time, effort, and resources devoted to the current practice in testing.

Imagine the potential benefit of taking all that time, energy and resources and devoting them with an equally concentrated effort to attract and train talented candidates to the teaching profession. We could resolve teacher shortages in math, science, English language learning, and special education. But, of course, this by itself is not a panacea. Simply increasing the ranks of our teachers is not enough to produce real change. But it would be a step in the right direction.

According to an article in EdWeek (April 14, 2022) summarizing the findings from the Merrimack College Teacher Survey conducted by the EdWeek Research Center during January and February 2022, barely half of the teachers surveyed are "satisfied" with their job and only 12 percent said that they are very satisfied, down from 39 percent in 2012.

More troubling, 44 percent of teachers said that they are likely to leave the teaching profession to take jobs outside education within the next two years. No one can expect us to improve our education systems without a well-educated, well-satisfied stable teacher workforce.

On top of what I would call a crisis of teacher dissatisfaction with their work, far too many of our students are not satisfied with their school experience. According to a 2009 survey of student engagement, as many as 66 percent of surveyed students cited being bored in every class or at least every day in school. These students said the primary reason for their boredom was the material being taught: 81 percent thought their subject material was uninteresting and 66 percent said that the material lacked relevance. As a school counselor, one of my responsibilities was to track kids who had not passed the exams they needed to graduate and to place them in remedial classes to help them pass the exams. In doing this work, I experienced many students' disengagement firsthand.

Passing standardized tests became the most important priority for teachers and students. Inevitably, teachers were encouraged to teach to the test. This was particularly true for schools where the majority of the students were living in poverty, children with learning disabilities, and ELL students. We have created a climate where students, families, and the public equate learning and education with passing tests. As a result, students spend an enormous amount of time getting prepared for the test at the expense of schools delivering an excellent curriculum. Arts, music, extracurricular activities, recess, educational field trips, school plays, and sports have all taken a back seat to test preparation. And yet we know that these are precisely the activities that are very important to students and contribute to motivation and engagement.

The impact that excessive testing has on teaching and learning became even clearer to me in Manchester, New Hampshire. When I met with a group of elementary teachers as the new superintendent, they expressed their frustration with too many assessments and a lack of freedom to make decisions about instruction in the classroom. A district-wide curricular pacing guide told teachers how to teach, the order in which the lessons will be taught, and when to give assessment tests to their students. I challenged all stakeholders to make changes to the pacing guide, and this resulted in more flexibility to principals and classroom teachers and reduced the amount of testing.

Given current education testing and standards requirements, it is not unusual for school district leaders facing pressure from federal and state policies to provide teachers with pacing guides that map out the topics to be covered before the spring testing dates. As was the case in Manchester and Rochester, it is not uncommon for the pacing guide to be driven by scripted lessons indicating when and how teachers must deliver them. Some of the most stringent pacing guides require that benchmark assessments be given every month, or every six weeks, dictating the amount of time to be spent on each topic. Pacing guides can go even further by specifying the number of minutes, periods, days, and weeks teachers should allocate for each topic. How in the world could a teacher working under these dictates successfully address the needs of a kid like me?

It is no surprise that this structure leads to teacher dissatisfaction and a desire to quit the profession. It also leads to students being less engaged the longer they are in school. In fact, it is my experience that the senior year of high school is the most wasted of all years. After being told that the most important thing for them is to pass the tests and meet the graduation requirements, it is no wonder that students "check out" and, as many of my students said, "take it easy" as soon as they meet these minimums. Too many of our students and adults confuse the meaning of education with graduation requirements and passing tests.

Parents, too, show little to no improvement in satisfaction with their children's education, according to a Gallup Poll in 2016, although there has been a significant increase in federal and state-level focus on education.

So how can we get from the current reforms that are contributing to the high level of dissatisfaction among students, families, and teachers to meaningful change? The reforms we live with today promised to provide qualified teachers for every child and to close the achievement gap. They have not achieved either goal. Continuing to do the things that are failing to produce progress does not make sense. So, let's get out of the rut.

Begin by redesigning the teacher's job duties. The goal would be to improve teacher working conditions and therefore retention, and to improve actual teaching and learning. Clearly, this will require the involvement of teachers and school leaders at the local level, which requires that they have the latitude to make changes without micromanagement from state and federal governments. Improving working conditions for teachers will improve the environment for students and all staff as well. One reason it is difficult to attract qualified teachers is that in many schools, particularly in urban or very rural districts, working conditions are dreadful. Studies show that working conditions are at least as important as salaries for attracting and retaining teachers who have other options. Poor leadership, lack of textbooks and curriculum materials, and poor facilities are some of the contributing factors to poor working conditions. Lack of teacher flexibility is also a significant factor.

So where can teachers and school leaders begin the discussion? Here are some suggestions:

First, we must acknowledge that the teacher's job is important to society and that it is highly stressful, especially when dealing with the most "needy" students—the students who need their teachers the most.

For most teachers, work does not start at 8:00 a.m. and end at 3:00 p.m. We need to look at the teachers' workload both in school and outside the school. I would suggest that many of the tasks required of teachers during the school day, such as lunch duty, hall duty, study hall duty, and such "invisible" tasks as making photocopies, could be fulfilled by individuals who do not need teacher-level qualifications and skills. Increasingly, given current testing regimes, teachers are required to do data analysis throughout the year that could be tasked to someone with specific expertise rather than taking the time from those who are trying to deal with kids. Visiting a school on my first day as superintendent in Rochester, I saw a line of teachers waiting to make photocopies. It struck me that we should and could do better than this and let teachers spend their first day on more critical things. Of course, this was an easy kind of problem: I knew what the problem was and I knew the solution. I informed teachers that from then on, the central office would print the materials they needed. Their time would be better spent getting to know their students and families at the beginning of the year.

Second, we can explore giving teachers more flexibility to improve teaching and learning. For example, in most of our schools everyone must show up at the same time and society presumes their day ends when the children leave. Teachers have extremely little flexibility regarding when and where they are required to be during the day; we are treating them like the children in our buildings. There may be ways to accommodate flexible working arrangements that allow teachers to have some latitude in their personal and professional lives, which could immediately improve their working conditions. I concur with Kat Howard (2020), who also believes that exploring a variety of flexible working arrangements can have a significant impact on the teaching staff and, I might add, on students as well by creating a better environment for teaching and learning.

Consider these questions: In the last five years, how many tasks and duties have been added to the teacher's plate and how many have been removed? Do you believe that all your job duties are well aligned with your skillset as a teacher or administrator?

People are often skeptical when I talk about such opportunities for improving teachers' work lives. Such skepticism is pervasive because there has been so much change in schools without meaningful, tangible results and, in some cases, with downright harmful results. I hear skepticism from teachers, administrators, scholars, students, policy makers, and people from the business community.

I hear that we've tried everything and "nothing has changed." This is ironic, since we are talking about constant change, but the reality is that the conditions for teaching and learning are not better. I hear that teachers' unions are the problem, that families are the problem, that politicians are the problem. When there is such a pervasive fixed mindset throughout an organization and community, it can appear to be impossible to influence meaningful change.

I realize that it takes more than just a growth mindset to achieve meaningful changes such as improving working conditions and the teaching and learning environment, but it does take that mindset.

Without the mindset that believes in the possibility, it cannot be achieved. And I'm not talking about the mindset of a single individual—I mean at least a group of individuals who trust each other and are dedicated to making something happen in their district. As Margaret Mead said on this issue: "Never doubt that a small group of thoughtful, committed citizens can change the world. Indeed, it is the only thing that ever has." Indeed.

Whatever little success I achieved as a school leader I attribute to my positive and hopeful attitude about change. In my first year in Manchester, New Hampshire, I faced a $5 million budget gap and everyone thought the only way to close it was by laying off 120 teachers. In my assessment, this solution would harm kids, further damage an already low morale in the schools, and decrease families' confidence in our school system because they had seen programs and services reduced year after year. Class size was unacceptably high, particularly in the elementary and middle schools. There were 30 students in some kindergarten classes.

I proposed a plan that did not require layoffs. First and foremost, we needed to override the city's tax cap to generate an additional $3 million to close the budget gap. No one—the school board, the mayor, the leaders of the board of aldermen, my administrative team—thought this could happen because it had never been done. The tax cap override would require approval from 10 city council members. The mayor did not support it. Only the parents were hopeful because they knew the consequences of failure. I was able to recruit two school board members to work with me on this plan.

Second, to address the board's concern about the budgetary impact of carrying the expense of underutilized space, I recommended moving the district's central administration office from a costly renovated historic building to unused space in one of our school buildings. This step helped save an important neighborhood high school, located in the poorest area of the city and serving mostly refugee students. And third, I deferred technology expenses to help close the budget gap.

I worked steadily with all stakeholders and decision makers for five months and, finally, our plan passed—to the great surprise of all. This could not have been accomplished without the extraordinary work of dedicated colleagues and supporters of the school district who believed in the plan. My leadership set the course with the support of this "small, thoughtful, committed" group of people.

When dealing with complex challenges in education, there is never a panacea. It is not possible to resolve all the issues that teachers and other educators confront because there are so many external factors beyond the control of teachers that influence the educational outcomes of our children. For example, student achievement is strongly correlated with the presence or absence of poverty, health, nutrition, parental support, and dysfunctional bureaucracies and school systems. But there are significant factors that teachers and other educators do have power to influence, such as curriculum, instruction, assessment, student–teacher relationships, high expectations, low expectations, fixed or growth mindset, and choosing appropriate pedagogical approaches. Most significantly, teachers and educators have the capacity to see harmful policies or practices in their schools and the choice to work to change them. All these areas, of which they have control, can have powerful influence on student academic performance and well-being.

Too often I hear teachers and other educators expressing discouragement in their work because they are confronting the limit to what they can do for their students given the number of outside influences that impact student outcomes. I am concerned when I hear teachers who sound like they have already quit without realizing it. I do my best to respond with compassion. I share my own background to tell them that even with my family circumstance, and barriers of language and social class—basically my story of growing up as a poor peasant boy in a poor third-world country—here I am talking about educating students as a superintendent of schools.

I am living proof that teachers who, despite all these challenges, make it possible for millions of kids like me to succeed against the odds. I like to point out that the millions of kids like me, from past generations as well as today, would not reach their potential without public education. The public education system in the United States is far from perfect but has achieved extraordinary gains on behalf of students, families, and our society.

As a superintendent of two urban districts, the success I experienced was due to innovation grounded in the local reality of what we were facing. The key is responding to that local reality and needs.

For example, in Rochester, New York, after 10 years of attempting to reform one of our largest high schools, the state Education Department designated it a failing school based on lack of improvement, and it was scheduled for closure. The district had already experienced this ineffective process of closing and reopening schools, known as "phase-in and phase-out." This included letting all staff go and reconstituting the school with a new design and staff. Because of the pain this caused students, families, teachers, and staff, and the lack of positive results, I ended this practice and looked for alternatives.

I researched our options and proposed that we pursue having some of our schools run by colleges, universities, or teachers. I had conversations with every area college president and the president of the teachers union asking for their collaboration. Although there was initial reluctance from college presidents, the University of Rochester eventually stepped up to manage East High School, independent of the dysfunctional district bureaucracy. In about five years this school improved its graduation rate from 29 percent to almost 70 percent. Notably, a significant number of East High School students were ELL or special education students.

Another example of innovation was our program to respond to the serious problem of summer learning loss facing ELLs and children in poverty. In the Rochester district, our children received the least amount of instructional time of any group of students in the county, a county where most of the students in districts outside the city live in middle- and upper-income families. In a high-poverty district like Rochester, students need more instruction time and support than students in higher-income districts, where most families are able to provide higher levels of support at home.

Under my leadership we worked to change this sad reality by addressing more and better learning time. We added 200 hours of optional instruction time at 13 schools where teachers voted for the program, using the "living contract" clause with our unions. We offered the kind of enrichment programs middle-class families take for granted. We partnered with cultural institutions and community-based organizations to provide after-school opportunities. We capitalized on the model of Horizons National (https://www.horizonsnational.org/about/), a pioneer in enrichment programs, whose mission is to "advance educational equity by building long-term partnerships with students, families, communities, and schools to create experiences outside of school that inspire the joy of learning." We built a program that offered city children fun, safe, and educational activities during the summer months. This did not happen with the wave of a wand, it required engagement by the community and by district teachers who wanted to participate to help implement and resource the new efforts. In the end, it was their project.

I participated in another innovative community-wide effort in the Manchester, New Hampshire school district that demonstrates the crucial role community can play in education. When I arrived in Manchester, the existing school district strategic plan was not well supported. There was enough controversy about it in the community that I realized we needed greater consensus before we could make any significant change in the school system. There was actually a great deal of interest and concern from the community leadership about the educational decline they saw. We were able to harness this interest to convene community and business leaders to undertake a serious attempt at developing a strategic plan that would include the entire community and the entire district workforce. More than 5,000 community members shared their views and aspirations for the district. I proposed that the plan be co-constructed by the district and the community. This eventually produced a new community organization, called Manchester Proud, that worked in collaboration with the district to develop a bold strategic plan that was accepted by the Board of School Committee in 2020. This innovative collaborative approach to developing a district plan helped to create significant buy-in that would ensure lasting stability. Manchester Proud continues to play an important role in the school district to this day.

Also in Manchester, we extended and deepened a partnership with the city's Boys and Girls Club, which provided case management services to at-risk students and their families. We broke down the silos that are typical in school districts by providing daily access, with parental consent, to information about at-risk students enrolled in the program, including student attendance and discipline data. This required the presence of trust and respect among all parties involved, all with the desire to support the needs of our students. Under the leadership of the Boys and Girls Club CEO, Diane Fitzpatrick, the organization established the "ABC program" to provide enhanced case management strategies for at-risk students. Now, attendance, behavior, and course completion were a shared effort with the community.

I offer these innovations from my own experience as illustrations of how new approaches to problems can lead to fresh solutions and remove longstanding barriers for the benefit of our students. However, I would not be surprised to learn that you have experienced innovation fatigue. For the past 20 years, we have been calling everything that is thrown at us "innovation" without any of it truly being innovative. For example, adding more testing, more standards, more computers, changing curriculum, and changing textbooks have all been referred to as innovative approaches. Different people assign different meanings to innovation. I have adapted the following key components for innovation in learning from the work of Murphy and colleagues (2014). Innovations in learning can solve problems and add value if they:

- Provide fresh solutions or remove traditional barriers to existing, articulated challenges in teaching and learning (and add value by building capacity for implementation);
- Identify a previously undetected need or barrier, then enhance the teaching and learning process with a novel solution (and add value by understanding the limiting factor in a new way and responding accordingly);
- Introduce new possibilities to enhance the teaching and learning process (and add value by providing new, more efficient opportunities for obtaining better results); and
- Allow the education system to adjust to new avenues through which students learn (and add value by capitalizing on and directing student use of technology). (p. 5)

And to these four criteria I would add a fifth:

- In addition to this list, I believe a fifth is necessary to carry out the kind of education innovation that doesn't simply add to practices and tasks, but subtracts ineffective practices and tasks, multiplies the delivery of better practices and tasks, and divides the workload of effective practices and tasks.

Although innovation is necessary, it is not sufficient to address all of the complex challenges in education. However, I believe that significant improvement in learning cannot be achieved without innovation being an integral part of our strategies. But considering everything we keep adding to the pile, without actually innovating, it is no wonder teachers, students, administrators, and families suffer from innovation fatigue. I offer the framework as one way to pivot from fatigue to focus on true innovation to improve teaching and learning.

Innovation is very often perceived as adding programs, services, resources, facilities, and so forth. Always adding. But there is a different way to do this in which you can incorporate a framework for innovation that includes not only, and not principally, addition, but also, and perhaps just as likely, subtraction, multiplication, and division to a mix that will avoid the kind of chaos created by simply adding and adding more.

My experience with the Boys and Girls Club in New Hampshire is an example. By expanding our collaboration with the agency, we created an additional entity to work with students and families in three areas important to student success—attendance, behavior, and course completion. Before we formalized this higher level of collaboration, the agency, which was already engaged in helping at-risk students, received student data quarterly and only on paper. Once we expanded the boundaries of sharing the data, technology allowed us to provide the information automatically on a daily basis; therefore, we subtracted manual steps and subtracted time from the process so intervention could happen immediately. Definitely a win-win. This expanded capacity also multiplied the engagement with students and families, which makes it more likely for students to succeed. Definitely the end-goal. This innovation could be viewed through the lens of divide and conquer. The tasks are now divided between the community and the schools. Each entity has less on its plate, but the students and families receive more services.

Some of the greatest challenges for teachers in urban districts are student attendance, discipline, and successful course completion. This is particularly true for those who teach our most vulnerable students, including ELLs. Think of the non–Spanish-speaking teacher of a Spanish-speaking student. Could a collaboration like the one we established with the Boys and Girls Club in Manchester be applied here? I don't see why not. In Rochester, New York, I was able to secure assistance from the Monroe County Department of Social Services, the Hillside Scholarship Program, and even a church, all of which served Spanish-speaking students and children living in poverty. The district shared student data, with parental consent, and the organizations addressed chronic attendance, discipline, and course completion issues. In another collaborative effort in Rochester, community members joined district staff to visit the homes of students with chronic attendance issues. This monthly "Attendance Blitz" allowed us to pair Spanish speakers with the homes of Spanish-speaking families to communicate the importance of attendance and address issues preventing the students from attending.

If there is one thing I hope you take away from these examples of innovation, it is that common sense innovation can, indeed, work. And if I can leave you with one overriding challenge, it is this: I believe that the most effective way to improve outcomes for our students is to improve the lot of teachers. We need to remake the job for the better. I believe this can be done.

I believe that teachers and administrators can take action to improve working conditions, in the schools and school systems where they work. Using common sense innovation based on your experience, your research and observation, your practice, and, most important, based on the current and future needs of your students, I would encourage you to use the checklist I've given here for evaluating education innovation and begin to think of the things that you can subtract, add, multiply, and divide in your vision of a redesigned teacher's job and for the profession as a whole.

Teachers can make meaningful changes in their organizations to produce better working conditions, leading to better teaching and learning environments and better outcomes for students, particularly those students least able to make their own way toward success without the undivided caring attention of their teachers. You can make change when you work on a small scale in your local school and district, from the ground up, admitting new ideas and by persisting in the effort. To fail to act on your own and your students' behalf would be to give up on common sense.

Changing the working conditions of teachers for the better is a necessary and urgent step toward addressing current teacher shortages, teacher retention, and our ability to attract enough talented people to join the profession. To effectively provide high-quality education for every K–12 student in America we must address the impediments to improving the teaching profession. As Adam Urbanski, president of the Rochester Teacher Association, wrote in 1998, "What impedes effective teaching is not that teachers are the problem; it is that teachers work within outmoded, unprofessional systems" (p.449).

That was a quarter of a century ago and, sadly, it is even more the case now. Despite all the changes in our society, the teacher's job remains woefully outmoded. The current state of the teaching profession cannot meet the increasing needs of diverse student populations, extraordinary increases in standards, and intense accountability standards. Policy makers at the federal, state, and local levels should focus on collaboration with teachers and other appropriate stakeholders to redesign the teacher's job and the teaching profession. Start by assessing the inflexible nature of the teaching job itself; teacher preparation programs; compensation compared with other professions; collaboration versus isolation; teachers' workload; and professional accountability versus external accountability, time, and support.

Transforming the teacher's job and the profession as a whole will take courage, collaboration, and innovation, but it can be done. The ultimate result will be a K–12 education system better able to meet the needs of students, teachers, administrators, families, and communities.

Most of us who have been part of this long stretch of top down educational reform are understandably exhausted. However, for the sake of our students and our profession, we cannot lose faith in the power of possibility to improve our school system to impact the lives of our students. Fortunately, no one gave up on me when the system and society might have, and therefore, I never gave up on myself. Remember the opening quote in this chapter, "If something isn't blatantly impossible, then there must be a way of doing it."

Reflect and Imagine Activity

Think about this seemingly simple framework that I call my Checklist Manifesto for educational innovation.

- Is your school involved in education innovation?
- Is the innovation being done by subtracting?
- Is the innovation being done by dividing?
- Is the innovation being done by multiplying?
- Are you suffering from innovation fatigue?

For example, a school principal might remove the lunch duty from all teachers to allow for teachers to spend more time on instruction issues and less on administrative duties, and to implement a team approach. Teachers share in teaching, planning, discussing students' work, adjusting instruction to meet student needs, and providing individual support to students, and the team shares responsibility for all the students they serve. This is an example of innovation by subtraction, addition, multiplication, and division.

Has your experience with innovation included both adding and subtracting? Can you think of ways to improve your classroom or your school by dividing up the way a task is done through collaboration to improve the students' and teachers' well-being?

Imagine that your superintendent and teachers union agree that in order to significantly improve teaching and learning and to attract and retain teachers, particularly in schools serving large numbers of ELLs, special education students, and students from low economic backgrounds, the outmoded teaching job description needs to be redesigned. Then you are given eight weeks to come up with a draft proposal for a new teacher job description to present to the school board. You lead a team of five teachers for this task. Write a draft of your vision for the new job description and discuss it with your colleagues in anticipation of presenting it to the superintendent and the teachers union.

References

Darling-Hammond, L. (2004). From "Separate but equal" to "No Child Left Behind": The collision of new standard and old inequalities. In D. Meier & G. Wood (Eds.), *Many children left behind: How the No Child Left Behind Act is damaging our children and schools* (pp. 3–32). Beacon Press.

Darling-Hammond, L. (2010). *The flat world and education: How America's commitment to equity will determine our future.* Teachers College Press.

Every Student Succeeds Act of 2015, 20 U.S.C. § 6301 (2015). https://www.congress.gov/bill/114th-congress/senate-bill/1177

Health Professions Educational Assistance Act of 1963, Pub. L. 88-129 (1963).

Howard, K. (2020). *Stop talking about wellbeing: A pragmatic approach to teacher workload.* John Catt Educational.

Kurtz, Holly. "A Profession in Crisis: Findings From a National Teacher Survey," *Education Week*, April 14, 2022, https://www.edweek.org/research-center/reports/teaching-profession-in-crisis-national-teacher-survey.

No Child Left Behind (NCLB) Act of 2001, Pub. L. 107-110, 20 U.S.C. § 6319 (2002).

Ravitch, D. (2014). *Reign of error: The hoax of the privatization movement and the danger to America's public schools.* Vintage Books.

Redding, S., Twyman, J., & Murphy, M. (2014). What is an innovation in learning? In Murphy, M., Redding., & Twyman, J. (Eds.), *The handbook on innovations in learning* (pp. 3–14). Information Age Publishing.

Saad, L. (2016). "Five Insights Into U.S. Parents' Satisfaction With Education". Gallup News, August 25, 2016, https://news.gallup.com/poll/195011/five-insights-parents-satisfaction-education.aspx.

Urbanski, A. (1998). Teacher professionalism and teacher accountability: Toward a more genuine teaching profession. *Education Policy*, 12(4), 449–457.